ANGEL DETOX

ALSO BY DOREEN VIRTUE AND ROBERT REEVES, N.D.

<u>Books</u>

Nutrition for Intuition (available June 2015)
Living Pain-Free
Flower Therapy

<u>Oracle Cards (divination cards and guidebook)</u>

Flower Therapy Oracle Cards

★

ALSO BY DOREEN VIRTUE

<u>Books/Calendar/Kits/Oracle Board</u>

Earth Angel Realms
The Big Book of Angel Tarot (with Radleigh Valentine)
Angels of Abundance (with Grant Virtue)
Angel Dreams (with Melissa Virtue)
Angel Astrology 101 (with Yasmin Boland)
Assertiveness for Earth Angels
How to Heal a Grieving Heart (with James Van Praagh)
The Essential Doreen Virtue Collection
Archangel Daily Messages 2015 Calendar
The Miracles of Archangel Gabriel
Mermaids 101
Mary, Queen of Angels
Saved by an Angel
The Angel Therapy® Handbook
Angel Words (with Grant Virtue)
Archangels 101
The Healing Miracles of Archangel Raphael
The Art of Raw Living Food (with Jenny Ross)
Signs from Above (with Charles Virtue)
The Miracles of Archangel Michael
Angel Numbers 101
Solomon's Angels (a novel)
My Guardian Angel (with Amy Oscar)
Angel Blessings Candle Kit (with Grant Virtue; includes booklet, CD, journal, etc.)
Thank You, Angels! (children's book with Kristina Tracy)
Healing Words from the Angels
How to Hear Your Angels
Realms of the Earth Angels
Fairies 101
Daily Guidance from Your Angels
Divine Magic
How to Give an Angel Card Reading Kit
Angels 101
Angel Guidance Board
Crystal Therapy (with Judith Lukomski)
Connecting with Your Angels Kit (includes booklet, CD, journal, etc.)
The Crystal Children
Archangels & Ascended Masters

ANGEL DETOX

Taking Your Life to a Higher Level
Through Releasing Emotional,
Physical, and Energetic Toxins

DOREEN VIRTUE &
ROBERT REEVES, N.D.

HAY HOUSE, INC.
Carlsbad, California • New York City
London • Sydney • Johannesburg
Vancouver • Hong Kong • New Delhi

Published and distributed in the United States by: Hay House, Inc.: www.hay house.com® • *Published and distributed in Australia by:* Hay House Australia Pty. Ltd.: www.hayhouse.com.au • *Published and distributed in the United Kingdom by:* Hay House UK, Ltd.: www.hayhouse.co.uk • *Published and distributed in the Republic of South Africa by:* Hay House SA (Pty), Ltd.: www.hayhouse.co.za • *Distributed in Canada by:* Raincoast Books: www.raincoast.com • *Published in India by:* Hay House Publishers India: www.hayhouse.co.in

Cover design: Steven Williams • *Interior design:* Tricia Breidenthal

Library of Congress Cataloging-in-Publication Data

Virtue, Doreen, date.
   Angel detox : taking your life to a higher level through releasing emotional, physical, and energetic toxins / Doreen Virtue, Robert Reeves.
      pages cm
   Includes bibliographical references.
   ISBN 978-1-4019-4431-5 (hardback)
   1. Mind and body. 2. New Thought. 3. Detoxification (Health) I. Reeves, Robert, N.D. II. Title.
   BF161.V57 2014
   131--dc23

                                    2013034473

Tradepaper ISBN: 978-1-4019-4258-8

12 11 10 9 8 7 6 5 4
1st edition, January 2014

Printed in the United States of America

To all of you who wish to attain higher energy and greater health.

CONTENTS

INTRODUCTION TO DETOX

Detox, or *detoxification,* is the process of removing unhealthy substances and energies from your life. Within these pages, we focus on physical, emotional, and spiritual detox methods. As your spirituality heightens, you'll be guided to release anything that no longer serves you, which may include foods, beverages, friendships, relationships, careers, and environments. Throughout this book, we share healing methods that can help you detox your life, which will enable you to experience greater joy.

You deserve to be happy, as we all do, since each of us is born with the same potential for happiness and success. By clearing away the fog of toxins, you'll be able to plainly see the path ahead. And by working with natural remedies under the watchful eyes of the angels, you will most likely enjoy the process of detoxification.

Detox is often thought of as a purely physical exercise. It conjures up images of cathartic and purgative treatments that rapidly and harshly remove unwanted substances from the body. But this doesn't have to be the case. The loving guidance of the angels provides you with simple, effective, and safe methods for improving your well-being. By letting go of anything that no longer serves you, you open yourself up to the joy and peace you're entitled to.

So be willing to release physical and emotional toxins from your life! Let the angels work with you as you proceed on your healing journey. You'll feel lighter, freer, and happier as a result.

Why Detox?

When you arrive on Earth, you're only given one body. This is the vessel that carries your soul for the duration of this lifetime. Your precious body is your primary tool for fulfilling what you came here to do, and you must care for it, as it cannot be replaced. When you're born, you commit to sacred contracts for your life purposes. As you progress through life, you'll uncover what those purposes are. They fall into two categories: *personal* and *global.*

Everyone is born with an individual, personal purpose. This may be learning compassion, healing grief, becoming comfortable with receiving, accepting forgiveness, and so forth. But global purposes aren't issued to everyone. These are for those who have a mission that benefits the lives of others and may include being a healer or spiritual teacher, writing books, helping the environment, inventing a new product, or being an advocate for those who can't speak up for themselves.

It's your job to complete your purpose within the space of this lifetime. If not, you may be sent back to Earth to learn the same lessons again. By completing your Divine mission, you'll be rewarded with greater happiness and love.

Detoxing your life from lower energies and unhealthy substances allows you to more clearly hear the voice of the Divine— such as God, Jesus, your Higher Self, and your angels. You'll start to hear these messages very clearly, which will help you discern what your life purpose involves so that you can take guided action as you progress on your path.

Detoxing improves your own well-being, and potentially helps other people as well, as you will become an inspiration to them. By walking your talk, you'll show others that true health is possible. Additionally, with the energy boost that detoxing gives you, you'll have the motivation to fulfill your purpose and provide help to others in a big way.

The ego voice tells you that it's too difficult to let go of old habits. The ego says that you need certain substances, foods, and toxic situations in order to stay "happy" and "secure." It tells you that if you detox, you'll become depressed, lose friends, and collapse in a heap.

However, the angels and God love you very much and only want the best for you. So please listen to your Higher Self as it guides you along the path of detoxification. The angels are helping you accomplish this right now.

There are many inherent pluses involved in detoxing. The primary one is that you'll feel a genuine state of wellness. Other benefits include increased clarity and vitality, heightened intuition, greater self-acceptance, emotional cleansing, abundant energy, and improved overall health.

What to Expect from a Detox

During the process of detoxification, your body removes "toxic waste." Your detox experience will depend on how much chemical and toxic buildup you've accumulated. An Angel Detox takes into account your sensitive nature, combining energetic clearing methods with naturopathic therapies.

If you're familiar with a standard store-bought detox kit, you'll notice definite differences with the Angel Detox. Many retail detox packs or cleanses contain laxative herbs and nutrients to increase your bowel function. You think that your body is going through a wonderful cleanse, but in reality, this type of detox is very limited. A standard detox ignores your energy, emotions, and environment. You'll find a holistic approach the most suitable for your sensitive soul. Plus, it addresses toxins from *all* areas of your life! In addition, highly sensitive people find a standard detox uncomfortable. We want you to *enjoy* your detox experience!

In the early stages of detoxing, you might experience headaches, fatigue, anger, frustration, and an increase in bowel movements; and you may have some issues with your skin as your body releases toxins. The reason for these short-lived encumbrances is the circulation of waste. Your body has to get the toxins moving before it can clear them out of your system.

Energetically, the liver is where you house anger. So, as the liver is kicked into action, you may feel temporarily moody. As long as you continue with your detox, you'll find that these symptoms dissipate rapidly. Generally speaking, they'll only last for a couple of days, but if they persist, consult with your local naturopath to make sure that your detox is balanced.

★

Take time to sit down and have heart-to-heart conversations with the angels. Archangel Raphael (the Healing Angel) will join Archangel Michael (the Angel of Strength and Courage) as you undergo your detox. Write down your thoughts, feelings, and questions in a journal; and consult with the angels on any concerns you have. You might start with: *What else can I do to enhance my detox?* or *Why am I experiencing headaches today?* Wait for your Higher Self to provide you with the answers.

Anything that you see, hear, feel, or think is a Divine message from the angels. Make notes so you can reread them at a later date. You'll see that your communications with the angels become clearer as you proceed. The messages that come through may be long and detailed, or you might receive small and succinct communiqués that have deep and profound meanings. But no matter what type of message you receive, know that the angels are watching over you during the entire process and want you to succeed!

What the Angels Say about Detoxing

You, like everyone, have guardian angels with you at all times. They are nondenominational guides assigned to you as part of your creation. Angels are part of human physiology, like a heart or liver; and they're committed to helping you live a long, healthy, and happy life. Your angels are invested in you and the fulfillment of your purpose.

For this reason, you may hear or feel your angels nudging you to detox. This may come in the form of repetitive thoughts or feelings urging you to give up toxic behaviors. You may shrug off this guidance because it's inconvenient, or it seems contrary to your prayers for a better career, relationship, and so forth, but we urge you not to do this.

Know that both of us have also received and followed this type of guidance with great success. Watching our friends, family, clients, and students deal in various ways with their inner guidance to detox, we have found that:

- Some people ignored it.

- Some delayed it.

- Some tried to bargain or negotiate with the guidance ("I'll give up this, but not that").

- Some argued with it.

- A few chose to follow it.

In the latter case, we've watched lives transform rapidly. For example, one of our friends saw all of his career dreams come true once he finally surrendered and followed his inner guidance to quit drinking alcohol and coffee, go vegetarian, and give up two toxic relationships.

You, too, can receive clear guidance from your angels by asking them, on a regular basis: "What changes would you like to see me make in my life right now?" Notice the feelings, thoughts, and visions you get right away . . . even if you don't like what you receive (for example, a message to give up your favorite food). Remember: your angels have been with you your whole life, and they know you better than anyone. All they want for you is your good health, happiness, and peace.

If you're unsure that you've accurately heard your angels, say:

"Angels, please give me a clear sign in the physical world that I will easily notice and understand to let me know that I've correctly heard you."

Once you know that your angels are guiding you to detox from a substance, relationship, or situation, say to them:

"Angels, please give me the courage to make this change in a healthful and harmonious way."

By working with the angels, you can also lose cravings so that there's no willpower involved. I (Doreen) was able to stop drinking alcohol and coffee and stop eating animal products and refined sugar because the angels completely eliminated my desire for these items. The same has happened to many other people, and it can happen for *you* if you ask for the angels' help.

The angels can't violate your free will, and can only help you if you ask. It doesn't matter *how* you ask for help, but only that you *do* ask for help: You can ask God directly for assistance; you can pray to Jesus or a saint; or you can visualize, affirm, or write your request. Your prayer can be a supplication (an appeal for help) or affirmative (thanking the Divine ahead of time for assisting you). All communication with the Divine that is sincere and love based works.

Letting go of addictions, unhealthful lifestyle habits, and unbalanced friendships heightens your connection to the angelic realm, as you'll release the psychic fog created by toxins. This fog stems from chemicals and negative energies, so the angels urge you to let this go. By working with the angels, you'll find that your appetite for healthful, nutritious foods will increase, and you'll become aware of how your body reacts to artificial substances. You may want to try a vegetarian diet for a week, or you may feel drawn to freshly squeezed juices. All of these examples are ways in which the angels are answering your prayers.

Sometimes you may accidentally ignore the angels' guidance, so definitely ask them for help in hearing the messages you're supposed to take to heart. Or, you can ask them how your detox can be more successful. You'll find that they will reply with dietary or lifestyle advice. The angels know how you can benefit most right now, and by following their messages, you'll be led to a path of absolute joy.

The Life Force of Food

The angels classify foods and drinks according to how they impact your vital energy and inner light. Natural, fresh, and organic fruits and vegetables have the highest vibrations, as they are both nutritious and are also filled with an inherent vibrancy. The sunshine that they absorb is held within their cells. As you consume these foods, your body welcomes the healing energy of the sun, and you begin to glow and grow radiant.

Processed and artificial "foods" have the lowest vibrations. These items serve no benefit to your body or energy. Similar to the nonnatural way they're produced, they provide you with an artificial sense of energy or satisfaction, and your body receives no reward for taking them in.

Even lower on the energy scale are those foods that contain, or are grown with, pesticides ("-cide" comes from the Latin *caedere,* which means "to kill") and have very low vibrations. Genetically modified (often called GM, GMO, or GE) foods have herbicides and pesticides grown into them, so they're the lowest-vibrational items of all.

At the time of this book's publication, genetically modified foods are unlabeled in the United States and Canada (in other countries, GMOs must be labeled). So, the only way to avoid GMOs in North America is to buy certified organic versions of the following foods:

The angels guide us to eat and drink organic foods, which are harvested without the use of chemicals and pesticides. Organics are also usually grown with love, by farmers who care more about health and the environment than profit. Animals on organic farms typically lived better lives; ate organic feed; and produced higher-energy milk, eggs, and flesh.

The ego tries to trick you by telling you that organic foods are more expensive. When comparing the surface price of organic versus nonorganic food, it may appear more costly. For example, organic tomatoes might seem more expensive than the nonorganic ones, but you're paying for the tomatoes that *didn't* make it to the store. No chemicals are used, so some might be eaten by bugs. The ones that survived will be well worth the investment. Organic food tastes like food should.

Remember those times when you cut open a tomato and you could smell it? These days, conventionally grown tomatoes have little smell, taste, or texture compared to those of the past. This is what organic food is all about: going back to a natural way of growing and harvesting foods, which is more sustainable, as it involves working closely with nature.

The angels show us a vision of interconnectedness when farming. The butterfly and the bee pollinate the flower and allow the tomato to grow. Some tomatoes might become the home for caterpillars. This leads to the next generation of pollinating butterflies. If pesticides and chemicals are used to kill the caterpillars and bees, the cycle of growth stops. The angels ask us to respect the land and the way our food is created, and to give a few pieces to the creatures that help us live healthfully.

Your grocery bill will likely go down when you follow a natural diet. As you transition to healthy, fresh produce, you'll no longer crave expensive, processed meals. It's actually very cost-effective to eat in a wholesome manner.

The angels guide sensitive people to avoid or reduce eating animal products because the animals' treatment affects the energy of the meat, dairy, and eggs. When an animal suffers, that suffering energy (including adrenaline) goes into the animals' flesh, and this extremely low vibration passes into those who eat these products. However, some believe that blessing the product and thanking the animal it came from can raise the vibration and purify the energy.

Also, in the past, some indigenous peoples silently asked animals for permission before hunting and killing them. However, in those days, animals lived freely, and their capture was on a fair and level playing field. These days, unfortunately, animals lead torturous, confined lives and are slaughtered cruelly. That energy affects those who consume the resulting products.

A Naturopathic Perspective on Detoxing

Detox is a favorite word of naturopaths (holistic physicians who use natural agents to treat physical ailments). So much emphasis is placed on the liver and the miraculous work it does, and this one organ helps eliminate toxic materials from the body, concentrating them and then releasing them into the bowel for removal. The liver is one of the only human organs that can regenerate. This is because it's so essential to a fully functioning body.

Without a good, working liver, your body will circulate toxic chemicals that will make you feel weak and fatigued, and cause headaches. Often when people visit a naturopath with multiple health concerns, the first treatment is for the liver, as naturopaths look upon it as a major detox organ. It strengthens the other detox organs of the body, including the skin, kidneys, lungs, and bowels. Each of these systems has its own way of releasing toxins. When all of them are working synchronistically, your body clears itself. Each system processes and detoxes the chemicals you come into contact with.

Looking at you holistically, naturopaths address your emotional toxins, too. Detoxing from stress and drama has a huge effect on your overall well-being. By making a commitment to release *all* forms of toxins, you'll be guided to the perfect support team.

The "tools" naturopaths prescribe include herbal medicines, nutritional supplements, and lifestyle practices. When you visit a naturopath, an individual treatment plan will be created just for you. Your naturopath's training will also impact his/her treatment style. Naturopaths have their own personal philosophies on health, so the best thing to do is to consult with practitioners who treat you as a unique human being. Even better, find a naturopath who believes in angels. This person will nurture you as a sensitive soul and help you trust your intuition.

How Often Should You Detox?

Your diet and lifestyle habits will determine how often you need to detox. Eating organic, healthful foods and maintaining a regular exercise routine means that you may only need to detox once or twice a year. However, if you eat a lot of fast or processed foods, smoke cigarettes, consume items with sugar regularly, drink alcohol, or live in a polluted area, you might think about detoxing every two months.

As you detox, your body will happily let go of unhealthful foods and drinks. Cravings for coffee may be reversed, and you might no longer enjoy drinking it. If this happens, go with the flow of energy. Let yourself release the substance, and move into greater health.

People in certain occupations might find themselves working in environments with harsh chemicals and toxins—for example, painters, hairstylists, manicurists, artists, cleaners, military personnel, and mechanics. Due to the chemicals they're exposed to, workers in these fields would benefit by detoxing regularly.

Similarly, if you live in an area with industrial or military-generated pollution, detoxing frequently is advised. Auto exhaust, factory fumes, and geoengineering weather-modification spraying ("chemtrails" of aluminum and barium nanoparticles appearing as thick white stripes in the sky that bleed into a white, silvery sky to block out the sunlight) are toxins that need to be released for optimal health and energy levels.

As mentioned, individuals in these environments would do well to commit to regular detoxes—say, every two months to ensure health and happiness. We feel that detox is a way of life, so rather than allowing toxins to build up in the first place, avoid them altogether as much as possible.

Choose to live as healthy and chemical-free as you can. And please work with the energetic clearing methods and health tips found in this book all year long.

★ ★ ★

CHAPTER ONE

HEALING METHODS FOR A SUCCESSFUL DETOX

Throughout this book, we refer to specific spiritual healing methods, so this chapter, which is akin to the "Ingredients You Will Need" section of a cookbook, lists and describes them all in detail.

Read through each method to gain greater insight. Then, learn how each method can be applied in specific situations. Choose a number of these tools to support your overall health, or select just one. Make sure you trust your intuition, and ask the angels to give you signs that you're choosing the right options. You can use any or all of the following healing methods to enhance your detox.

Archangel Raphael's Addiction Release

Archangel Raphael provides a powerful clearing method for substances you're willing to release. Please reflect on whether you're ready to let these substances, foods, or beverages go. However, the healing still works even if you don't think you're ready yet. By acknowledging that your life would be better without dependency, you allow the angels to step in. When the angels give

1

you messages about which items to release, trust in these feelings and choose to let them go.

The angels ask you to release these addictions in order to bring you greater joy. Don't look upon this process as if you're *losing* something—you're not, you're *gaining!* Your Divine life purpose is an important mission that only *you* can complete. Therefore, God needs you to be in your healthiest state.

Find a quiet space to sit peacefully. Begin by breathing deeply, taking your breath all the way down to your stomach. Exhale fully and completely as you let go of tension. Continue this deep breathing for several minutes. Now visualize the foods, substances, and beverages that you'd like to release. See them sitting above your lap, hovering in front of your stomach area. You may clairvoyantly see thin, sticky fibers extending from your body to these items. They are cords of addiction that are anchoring the unhealthy items in your aura. Now call upon Archangel Raphael by saying:

"Archangel Raphael, please release me from these cords of addiction now. Please take these items out of my aura and into the light."

You may see or feel Raphael clearing your body. He uses a white, cleansing foam that dissolves the cords. As he releases the cords of addiction, remain in a relaxed state by breathing deeply. See or feel the unhealthy substances leaving your body and being dissolved into the light. Ask for Raphael's healing by saying:

"Raphael, please send your healing, emerald-green light into my stomach area. I know and trust that this will prevent cravings or desires for these substances in the future. Thank you."

Sense Raphael's healing light warming your abdomen. Visualize the unhealthy foods floating away. The angels now guide you to release those foods and substances in a gentle and supportive manner.

Archangel Michael's Spiritual Vacuuming

Vacuuming is a spiritual clearing method channeled from Archangel Michael. It's extremely effective for releasing negativity. Michael dispels psychic attacks and blocks by using his etheric suction tube, which resembles a vacuum. By inviting Archangel Michael into your life, you give him permission to help you. Ask him to vacuum your body, aura, or home and he will remove unwanted negativity for you. His tube also suctions away fear, and at the other end of the tubing is the Band of Mercy—a group of smaller angels who accompany Archangel Michael in his clearing work. They transmute all lower energies to a higher vibration and work to instill love and peace.

Call on Michael by saying:

"Archangel Michael, please be here with me now. I ask you to please vacuum [my body, my home, my office, the planet, etc.]. Please suction away the lower energy of fear. Release all darkness to awaken the light. I ask you to now lift away all traces of negativity, leaving behind only love."

See, in your mind's eye, Michael clearing away any negative energy. By doing so, he reveals the beauty of your Divine light. You can ask him to amplify or reduce the speed with which he suctions away fear. Ask him to switch the vacuum to low, medium, high, or extra high. Continue working with Michael until you feel that all traces of fear are removed.

Next, infuse the area with additional healing light:

"Michael, please send your pure, loving light of God into [my body, home, office, etc.]. Please protect me from lower energies and remind me to call upon you for guidance and support. Thank you."

Archangel Michael can be with everyone simultaneously. Call upon him for yourself, and also ask him to help loved ones who need clearing. Michael cannot interfere with others' free will, so he will only conduct healings if people are willing to receive them.

When you undergo a spiritual vacuuming, you raise your vibration, and as a result, you will crave higher-energy substances. So, this process helps you align yourself with natural, nutritious foods and drinks. You'll also find yourself aligning with like-minded individuals.

The angels are happy to clear you as often as you need it, and they may gently guide you to avoid situations causing you pain. By becoming a clean and clear vessel, you intensify your sensitivity. Soon you'll identify the situations or people that lower your vibration; and when you're around them, you may notice headaches, fatigue, constant yawning, itchy skin, or difficulty concentrating. Take these as signs from your angels to avoid these people and situations, as they're only causing you harm. Sometimes the most healing thing you can do is to extract yourself from unhealthy environments.

For example, you may find that you can no longer listen to, or be around, people who complain a lot or who create lots of drama. By releasing those individuals, you're not being a bad friend—you're merely attempting to raise your vibration. You're making the choice to only allow positive energies to come into your life.

You may feel guided to modify other types of relationships as well. This, too, is part of the natural process of developing your spirituality. For example, certain people might abuse alcohol and/ or drugs, which you realize is a form of self-harm. Many convince themselves that they're not addicted, and that they can stop anytime they like. But your inner knowingness and Higher Self tells you otherwise.

Trust this higher guidance. You're a beautiful example of God's love, and you have the ability to shine your light upon those in need, but you don't have to join them on a path of despair to do so. You can't help your friends if you involve yourself in their crises and dramas. Doing so will only create *more* people in need of healing.

Archangel Michael's Cord Cutting

Etheric cords are negative, or fear-based, attachments. They look like tubes connecting you to other people, places, or objects; and can make you feel tired and lose motivation. They're responsible for unexplained pain, so if there are no clear physical causes for your discomfort, it may be due to an etheric-cord attachment.

Many people have experienced instantaneous relief after cutting these cords, which can affect you by both transmitting and absorbing energy. These cords suction your energy and vitality and give it to others. Think of friends who are draining, or people who make you feel physically and mentally exhausted. This is due to fear-based cord attachments. These individuals are siphoning off your energy reserves in order to keep themselves going.

On the other hand, if the other party becomes angry or stressed, these emotions tumble down the cord to you, and you suddenly experience them for no logical reason. They may hit you quite suddenly and confuse your energy. One minute you're fine, and the next you feel intense anger or pain.

Cords frequently attach to helpers; so if you enjoy assisting others, or have a healing business of some sort, you may have formed etheric-cord attachments. That's why it's so important to cut your cords regularly. Otherwise, you may be overcome with negative attachments, which will drain you and make you feel chronically fatigued and burned-out.

From a clairvoyant standpoint, these cords look like tubes going from one person to another. They begin as thin, string-like cords. As time progresses and the relationship develops, the cords grow.

The underlying energy of cords can stimulate thoughts and feelings such as:

- *What if they aren't there the next time I need help?*
- *I'm jealous and want what they have.*
- *They made me feel so good. I must talk to them again to feel that way.*
- *I don't want them to leave me.*
- *I feel resentment toward them.*
- *They're the source of my power.*
- *They're the source of my healing.*

Archangel Michael severs the cords of fear, releasing you from the unhealthy part of the relationship. To start this process, find a quiet space and begin by breathing deeply. Consider lighting a white candle for purification. Or, you can sit in front of a bunch of white roses.

Start to bring your attention to your physical body. Begin by using your intuition. Notice anywhere that feel tighter or more restricted. Become aware of areas on your body that feel warmer than others. Next, take your dominant hand (the hand you naturally write with) and scan it around your aura. Again, pay attention to changes in air pressure, tingling, or heat. All of these sensations are clues that there are etheric-cord attachments. Call upon Archangel Michael by saying:

"Archangel Michael, please sever and release any cords of fear. I am willing to let go of this unhealthy, unbalanced energy. I choose instead to align myself with love and light. I ask you to remove any negative energies from my body. Please release all effects of these cords now. Thank you."

Follow Michael's energy as it scans your body. Be aware of the areas of tension that are being dissolved. You may receive flashes of people or situations that cords were connected to. Let these feelings move through your body, letting them go. This is all part of the detox process.

Archangel Michael will take excellent care of you and help you feel more comfortable. Remember, you can ask him for additional support at any time. By working with Michael, you will sever these cords of fear from your body. Relax, and allow him to do his work.

If you feel that certain cords weren't released, ask your angels why. They may show you images or give you feelings about the person connected to a particular cord. Visualize a peaceful conversation with this individual. Say everything that's on your mind and in your heart. You may get a sense of what this person would say in turn. When complete, tune in to your body again. Notice the subtle differences and the greater energy you now feel. You've successfully released a negative, unbalanced relationship! Tell the Universe that from this moment on, you will only accept loving people into your life.

CHAKRA CHART

Crown Chakra
Ear Chakras
Third Eye

Throat Chakra

Heart Chakra

Solar Plexus Chakra

Sacral Chakra

Root Chakra

Archangel Metatron's Sacred Beam of Light

Your chakras (your centers of life force and vital energy) are like sponges that absorb energy, some of which may not always be for your highest good. To ensure that you hold only positive and loving energies, it's a good idea to clear your chakras.

The following is a method offered by Archangel Metatron, who brings balance to all areas of your life. He works to correct the amount of work, rest, and play you partake in. He also brings an energetic and spiritual balance to your chakra system. Whenever you feel stuck, blocked, or clouded, ask Archangel Metatron for healing.

Find a quiet space and begin by breathing deeply. Close your eyes and relax. Call upon Metatron by saying:

"Archangel Metatron, please cleanse and balance all of my chakras using your Sacred Beam of Light."

Visualize a pure white beam of light coming down toward you from Heaven. Relax, and watch as Metatron guides this healing energy in through the top of your head. See or feel yourself filled with pure white light. Sense this energy filling all of your cells with the purity of angelic love. You may see ancient symbols being sent through the beam, so if you do, allow them to work their healing magic within your soul. You may recognize some of the symbols, and others may be new to you. It's not important for you to understand everything. Instead, trust in the angels and God.

Next, allow the beam to pass out through your root chakra, which is the area at the base of your spine (see illustration on facing page). Notice as it transforms into a ruby-red color. This red light clears away blockages and fully awakens your root chakra.

When the clearing is complete, Archangel Metatron will guide the beam out through your sacral chakra. Here, it takes on a vibrant orange. Feel the orange light dissolving all darkness and healing your sacral chakra.

Continue working with Metatron through the rest of your chakras:

- Solar plexus—yellow
- Heart—green and pink
- Throat—sky blue
- Third eye—dark blue
- Ear—red-violet
- Crown—purple and white

When you feel ready, thank Metatron for his healing by saying:

"Thank you, Archangel Metatron, for this healing and clearing. Please continue working with me as I release all old energies that have held me back. I am now ready to embrace my light and follow the guidance of God."

The more you work with this method, the smoother and faster it will become. Initially, it may take five minutes or more for each chakra center. With regular clearing, there's not as much stagnation and psychic debris to remove. So, you can eventually move through the entire process in just a few minutes. Metatron clears away negative energy whether you're aware of it or not. And, of course, as the Law of Free Will dictates, the angels must have permission before they can assist you.

Healing Crystals

Crystals are healing stones that carry an inherent energy within them. As your spiritual gifts awaken, you feel a gentle pulse of energy as you hold a crystal. They store and direct healing energies, which you can greatly benefit from. Your body easily absorbs their vibration. Sit with your crystal and set your intentions, which gives the stone a way to direct its love.

Some wonderful crystals and stones for detox include:

Amethyst: Provides protection from toxic energies.

Clear quartz: Great for a general detox of anything and everything.

Green stones (jade, emerald, malachite, etc.): Provide healing support.

Moonstone: Helps you release and let go.

Obsidian: Grounds you so that you don't feel spacy. Helps with focus and concentration.

Orgonite (metal shavings and quartz crystal set in resin): Protects you from geoengineering weather-modification aerial spraying of aluminum and barium nanoparticles ("chemtrails").

Rose quartz: Heals emotions and gives you hope and faith.

Smoky quartz: Wonderful for clearing away toxic relationship energy, especially with respect to people from your past.

You can wear, hold, work, or sleep next to these crystals to receive their healing support.

Crystals are sensitive tools that can easily absorb negative energies; therefore, it's best to cleanse your crystals the first time you bring them home. Also, cleansing is a nice little to show them that you appreciate them.

And, be sure to cleanse your stones if you haven't done so for some time. Think of how many times you walk past your crystals every day. Crystals are like sponges. Since they want to help, they clear heavy and lower energies from you. This is a lovely service that the crystals do for you, so cleansing them regularly is your way of repaying them for the healing they've been giving you unknowingly.

In addition, cleansing your crystals removes all past associations—that is, the energies of previous owners, countries, and environments, leaving behind pure healing energy. Crystals come from all over the planet and have endured being lifted from the Earth, miners sorting them, wholesalers packing them, retailers pricing them, and then finally making their way to you. They can be depleted and drained from their long journey.

The ancient Lemurians, a highly spiritual civilization that preceded Atlantis, worked closely with crystalline energies and learned effective methods of cleansing crystals. They recalibrated the crystals' energy so that it functioned at the best possible frequency and worked with the crystals' "internal circuit board." The Lemurians had a highly developed knowledge of how crystals worked. They easily and effectively corrected all energy imbalances and repaired any negative energy that the crystals may have absorbed.

To have the Lemurians cleanse your crystals today, simply call on them and ask them to do so by saying:

"Lemurians, please help me cleanse my crystals now. Refresh and intensify their energies so they may become tools used for my highest good.
Thank you."

There are many ways in which you can cleanse your crystals. Asking the Lemurians to cleanse them is just one method, but you can also try smudging, which is an old method of clearing energy that uses smoldering herbs, namely white sage, in order to lift energy.

★

Archangel Michael is excellent at clearing negative energies from your crystals, too. Call upon Michael by saying:

"Archangel Michael, I ask you to send your purifying energy into my healing crystals. Please awaken their inner knowledge to heal and inspire. Please prepare my crystals for healing work and align them with my energy now. Thank you."

Next, charge your crystals with positive energy. You can do so through prayer. Open your heart to the healing crystals and express your gratitude. Or, leave your stones in the light of the sun or moon for four hours.

Now, your crystals are ready to be programmed with your loving thoughts. To achieve this, work *with* the crystals. Speak to the stones as if they're loving friends, which they are. Pour your heart out and admit to any concerns or fears. Let the crystals know exactly what you hope for. Also, share your previous experiences. Include in your prayer that you're willing to accept something greater that God and the angels may bring. If they see an easier method for success, be open to it! You needn't use any special words or phrases to program your crystals; it's all about your intention. When your intention is pure, you'll receive the best possible outcome. Have the courage to step out of your comfort zone and speak from your heart.

Flower Therapy

Flowers are physical representations of love from our Creator. They serve as reminders of the Heavenly presence that surrounds us in nature.

As you go through your day, you might notice a single flower peeking out from a crack in the sidewalk. Or, you may observe some stunning blooms in a neighbor's garden. Previously you might never have noticed that they were there, yet today you're captivated by them. The angels say that in these cases, the flowers have been placed there just for *you*. It's part of their sacred purpose to heal you. And, as you acknowledge the presence of the angels and flowers, they are given permission to help you. So, take a moment to literally stop and smell the roses. Your mind will become clearer and more focused.

At times you may become overwhelmed with the chaos and drama of your everyday life. These feelings appear as a psychic fog within your aura. When you're encased in this fog, it's very difficult to tell which way is up, what direction is forward, and where you want to travel. First, you must lift this cloud away so you can clearly see the road ahead, and flowers can help you do so. By welcoming flowers into your environment, negative energy is instantly lifted.

To begin working with flowers, bring fresh blooms into your home. You can also plant them in your garden, or print pictures of them to display around your house or apartment. (To discover more healing ways to connect with the angels of nature, see our book *Flower Therapy*. We also discuss detoxing your emotions with flowers in Chapter 8.)

Tree Therapy

Trees are powerful healers and teachers for those who are sensitive enough to hear the voice of the tree. I (Doreen) sat beneath trees and wrote about their messages in my book *Healing with the Fairies*. I find that (like people) each tree has a specific life purpose. Some trees help boost confidence, others help with relationship issues, some help manifest abundance, and so forth. Just silently ask a tree about its purpose, and then trust the answer you receive in your mind.

Trees also perform physical healings. If you feel tired, ill, or injured, you can place your back against a tree (either sitting or standing). The tree will immediately begin absorbing toxins, pain, and low energies. You'll feel this process! And don't worry—this won't hurt the tree. Just as trees transmute carbon dioxide into fresh air, so too do they transmute and purify old pain energy.

Connecting with Nature

We saved one of the best detox methods for last: Mother Nature. A lot of toxins are accumulated because so many of us live and work indoors, which isn't natural for any creatures, including humans. We aren't meant to breathe air-conditioned air or work under artificial lighting. In fact, studies show that many modern illnesses came into being precisely at the time that artificial lighting became commonplace!

We need sunlight in moderation to trigger the brain's production of the feel-good chemical *serotonin*. Serotonin is also the precursor to melatonin, which the body needs in order to sleep, and repair itself. Without enough melatonin and serotonin, we wake up feeling tired, grumpy, and hungry for junk food.

We also need sunlight to ensure that we're getting adequate vitamin D in our system. Breast cancer and other serious diseases have been associated with vitamin D deficiencies.

The angels say that full-spectrum lighting is necessary for optimal health, and that the rainbow prism within full-spectrum sunlight feeds each of the colors within the chakra system (since it's a rainbow, also). So, for example, if you're having stomach issues or power struggles, the yellow light within the full-spectrum rainbow would support the healing of these issues, since yellow is the color of the solar plexus, which is associated with these issues.

While you never want to get sunburned, the opposite (avoiding the sun too much) is equally dangerous. Also, please read the ingredient lists on sunscreens carefully before applying them. Many of these products are loaded with toxic chemicals. Always be sure to choose organic sunscreens, available at your local health-food store or online.

In addition, the angels say that moonlight, starlight, sunsets, and sunrises also increase our overall wellness:

Sunset: The angels say that watching a sunset helps our chakras become relaxed, and prepares us for a good night's sleep.

Starlight: The angels say that being outside beneath the stars triggers our creativity, and helps us be more artistic.

Moonlight: Since ancient times, our ancestors have stood beneath the full moon as a powerful method of releasing everything that is toxic from their lives.

Sunrise: The angels say that watching a sunrise awakens the chakras, providing a natural boost of energy.

★ ★ ★

CHAPTER TWO

NOURISHING YOUR PHYSICAL BODY

The Angel Detox is an overall mind-body-spirit process. Let's focus on the physical body first.

Healing Digestion

A healthy, balanced digestive system absorbs the beneficial nutrition from the foods and beverages you consume. This is an automatic process that doesn't require conscious effort on your part. However, when something doesn't go according to plan, your digestive system slows down and you're no longer receiving the health-giving benefits of what you eat. You might experience symptoms such as bloating, constipation, diarrhea, or nausea. Each of these symptoms serves as a red flag that your digestion is in trouble. Perhaps it's not the most glamorous system of your body, but it's an essential component of your good health. Let's discuss the role of food allergies, leaky gut, and the mysterious irritable bowel syndrome (IBS).

Digestion starts in the mouth and relies on what you choose to eat. If you have a food allergy or intolerance, you'll likely experience digestive discomfort, coupled with heartburn/acid reflux. Food allergies are so prevalent but often overlooked. From a naturopathic perspective, food allergies/intolerances needn't cause severe reactions, such as anaphylaxis, to qualify as such. The body's response is often delayed by several hours, or even days. So it may be the glass of milk you had yesterday that's causing your symptoms today.

If you continue to eat foods your body is intolerant of, you'll continue to get symptoms. Your gut becomes inflamed, and rather than absorbing nutrition, it tries to fight against the food you eat. This leads you down a path of poor digestion and the various vitamin and mineral deficiencies that accompany it. So, be willing to release the foods that cause you pain in exchange for greater comfort and vitality.

Constant inflammation in your stomach due to food allergies can lead to a "leaky gut." Your digestive system becomes so weak that it no longer differentiates between good nutrition and toxins. As a result, your body starts to absorb both into the bloodstream. This leads to fatigue, exhaustion, and headaches, along with mood swings and anger. Toxins are floating around your body and causing you to feel unbalanced.

The first step is to eliminate all foods that your body dislikes. The second is to strengthen your gut. Taking the herbal medicine goldenseal can restore the lining of your digestive tract, and you might also consider a glutamine supplement to reduce inflammation and improve your gut's integrity.

A diagnosis of the puzzling condition *irritable bowel syndrome* (IBS) is confirmed by eliminating every other possibility. If you test negative for all other digestive issues, you may be diagnosed with IBS, characterized by irregular bowel habits with either constipation, diarrhea, or a combination of the two. If you're diagnosed with IBS, increase your fiber intake immediately. The easiest way to do so is to consume more fresh fruits and vegetables, which are naturally rich in fiber and help improve your elimination. Or, you can take slippery elm bark powder. Just ensure that you follow it with a glass of water to allow the powder to be absorbed.

Many IBS patients find that fresh vegetable juices work wonderfully, providing good nutrition along with soluble fiber. These juices will boost your energy levels and help soothe your gut. Symptoms of IBS are strongly linked to your nervous system and emotions. When you become stressed, the symptoms get worse. So take solace in relaxation activities such as meditation, tai chi, and yoga; and mist the aroma of lavender through your home to promote calmness. Even spending time with compassionate friends does a world of good.

Food Allergy Testing

A lot of troubling conditions such as swelling, skin issues, weight gain, and binge eating arise from food allergies and sensitivities. As foods become more contaminated with genetic modification and pesticides, allergies are increasingly common. But once you identify and stay away from the foods that your body is rejecting, the symptoms go away. Tests that can be taken to identify your allergies include the skin-prick test and blood tests. The skin-prick test can be performed by your doctor; however, this test often focuses on immediate immune responses such as pollen or pet dander. It may not be that useful for slower-acting food intolerances. Other options are blood tests that can be ordered through your naturopath. These measure your body's reaction to a wide range of foods, but are often expensive, as they're performed by private laboratories. However, the results can be highly informative, as they'll provide a list of the foods your body is struggling to cope with. They may also give you a scale of how affected you might be by certain individual items.

A simple way of identifying foods you're allergic to, or are intolerant of, is to make an educated guess. Which foods or beverages do you binge on? In other words, when you have one bite or drink, do you feel as if you can't stop? Bingeing is often a sign of an allergy.

People are often addicted to the foods that they're most intolerant of. So, if you crave and consume large amounts of dairy products, consider removing them from your diet for a week or two. Let's say, for example, that you have cereal with milk for breakfast, a cheese sandwich for lunch, a yogurt smoothie for an afternoon snack, and creamy pasta for dinner. Dairy is in all these meals, so you'll most likely see a significant difference when you cut back. After taking a break from dairy, you can reintroduce these products and again monitor your symptoms. If you notice an increase in symptoms over the first few days, then chances are your body is struggling to digest this food group, and it would be in your best interests to avoid dairy for several months to give your body a real rest. Or, after removing the dairy product initially, you may feel so good that you'll want to continue to avoid it. This is great, as it will show that you're listening to the urges of your body and the messages from your angels.

Also, notice any swelling, bloating, or itching that occurs after ingestion of a certain food or beverage, which are signs of a food allergy or sensitivity. Remove the food or beverage from your diet and determine whether the symptoms go away.

Remember that you can ask your angels to guide your food choices, and to steer you clear of allergens. They will also help you reduce or eliminate cravings for unhealthful foods.

The most common food allergies and sensitivities are related to:

- Milk
- Eggs
- Peanuts
- Tree nuts (cashews, walnuts, almonds)
- Fish
- Shellfish (crab, lobster, shrimp)
- Soy products
- Wheat/gluten

However, there are many other foods and ingredients that can cause health issues. Once you identify which food is giving you trouble, you'll need to vigilantly check ingredient labels and ask restaurants for details about food preparation and the contents of dishes.

The Importance of Water

Your body consists of 70 percent water. Interestingly enough, a similar percentage of water covers the surface of the earth.

Water is vital to keeping you healthy and happy. Through general metabolic processes, your body loses over 4.2 cups (a liter) of water each day. Therefore, you need to consume a reasonable quantity of good-quality water. This keeps your system working at an optimal level. Water is important for digestion, circulation, transporting nutrients, and removing wastes. As old toxins are cleared from your cells, you need water to wash them away. Adequate hydration prevents the negative compounds from becoming concentrated and causing you harm.

People often misconstrue thirst as hunger. They eat food rather than drink water. When you sense "hunger," tune in to your body and ask what this feeling truly is. Is your body asking for food, or is it saying that it needs more water? Often you'll find that you're really thirsty. Now you can quickly relieve the sense of hunger by drinking some water.

Without an adequate amount of water, it becomes difficult to concentrate, and you'll experience fatigue as your brain, which is made up of about 75 percent water, becomes dehydrated. The brain is the area of your nervous system that sends out the messages to your body. If you expect to function well during the day, you'll want to make your brain happy. When you become dehydrated, it's harder to think. When it becomes harder to think, it's harder to focus on positive and loving thoughts. You may find that your mood lowers as a result of dehydration. As this occurs, your connection to the angels becomes strained. So by keeping yourself hydrated, you'll enjoy light thoughts and a bond with the Divine world.

Natural springwater is best for your body. It doesn't contain any harsh chemicals or pollutants like regular tap water does, as it is taken straight from an underground spring and is virtually unprocessed. This leaves intact the minerals and trace elements (also known as microminerals) within the water, which your body needs. Water is such an essential ingredient in your body's functions that it's worth the investment to drink good-quality springwater.

Fluoride

Fluoride is a by-product of the phosphate fertilizer industry that was added to drinking water with the promise that it would prevent tooth decay. However, when comparing data from countries that have fluoridated water and from those that don't, there's no difference in the incidence of decay. Today, fluoride is understood to be a toxic heavy-metal by-product. Activists are demanding that their local water districts stop adding it into the water supply. The amount of fluoride in drinking water varies in different areas.

Warning labels are placed on many toothpastes because they contain fluoride. Each year, hundreds of children contract gastrointestinal issues due to the fluoride they've ingested via toothpaste. Yet, the amount of fluoride in a pea-size amount of toothpaste is similar to that contained in a cup of tap water. On the one hand, we're told to drink it; on the other, we're told to contact the poison hotline. We highly recommend avoiding fluoride in all forms. Instead, for your oral hygiene, look for natural, chemical-free toothpastes that don't contain fluoride or carrageenan (a common food additive made from algae or seaweed that's used as a binder, thickener, and stabilizer), which can cause inflammation.

Better yet, make your own chemical-free toothpaste from organic coconut oil, food-grade peppermint oil, and pure baking soda. These ingredients are readily available at health-food stores. Mix them to suit your own taste levels.

Fluoride is a toxin that can create joint pain, and affect the tissues of the thyroid and brain. It's a mutagen, which means that it causes genetic damage that may lead to cancer. Many studies have shown that fluoride affects brain function—lower levels of intelligence are linked with higher levels of fluoride. A number of studies have found that long-term exposure to fluoride (drinking fluoridated water) can damage the brain. And some have even suggested that there's a conspiracy behind the introduction of fluoride into drinking water—a topic you can research easily online and reach your own conclusions.

We recommend that you not ingest fluoride by avoiding regular tap water, fluoridated toothpastes, and processed foods and drinks so you don't ingest fluoride. The best way to remove fluoride from your drinking water is to either distill it or pass it through reverse osmosis, although it's unlikely you'll be able to distill water in your own home. You can purchase distilled water, but its energy is quite lifeless. However, you *can* have reverse-osmosis filtration systems fitted in your home. And, of course, you can avoid drinking fluoridated water altogether by purchasing natural springwater. But what type of water are you using to shower and bathe in? This water still may contain fluoride. A filtration system is an investment in your health and well-being.

Learn where your water is coming from and if it contains fluoride by contacting your local water district. You can also test your own water with kits that you can purchase online. If you choose to drink bottled water, find out the process used to collect it. You'll find that many springwaters are treated with chemicals and may contain just as much fluoride as regular tap water. Look for quality water that involves minimal handling. Find a brand that pumps the water from an underground spring and puts it right into the bottle.

Avoiding BPA in Plastic Bottles

Bisphenol A, or BPA, is a chemical used to make plastics stronger. Many water bottles and food containers contain BPA. These plastics will be labeled with a recycling number 3 or 7, but these numbers alone don't mean that the bottle is harmful. A 3 means that the plastic is made with PVC, and a 7 implies that it doesn't fit into any other category. BPA-containing plastics fit into both categories, but so do other plastics that may be safe.

BPA is linked to several health concerns, including hormonal imbalances, liver abnormalities, and poor development of the brain in infants, as well as diabetes, breast cancer, heart disease, and infertility. Always look for BPA-free products whenever you purchase plastics.

BPA bottles leach the chemical in to the water they carry. When they're heated, like being left in a hot car or the grocery store's warm storeroom, they leach even more of this hazardous material. So avoid plastic bottles that have a number 3 or 7 on them. We recommend buying drinking water from glass bottles. Brands such as Voss from Norway and Whole Foods Italian still water are examples.

BPA can also be present in canned foods, and the plastic lining of cans can be made from BPA plastic. Harvard professors found that after eating canned soup once a day for five days, you increase your levels of BPA by 1,000 percent because of this. The brand Amy's Kitchen guarantees that their canned food is BPA-free.

Even your toothbrush needs to be BPA-free, as you're putting this into your mouth two or three times daily. The brand Preserve, available for sale online and in health-food stores, is BPA-free. Preserve also has a recycle program where you send in your old toothbrushes postage-free, and the sterilized materials are then used to manufacture new toothbrushes.

★

Many reputable water companies provide at-home water dispensers. Do your research, as the bottled water you drink may not be very good. The water supplied by your office is probably just as poor. Check the mineral analysis and make sure it doesn't just have sodium and chloride. Some sodium is needed, but it shouldn't be the only mineral present. Good-quality water will also include small traces of calcium, magnesium, and potassium. With these minerals present, you'll be able to enjoy your water knowing your body can use it in metabolic functions.

Purified water and distilled water, which sounds good, means that all of the microminerals have been removed. This leaves you with just H_2O. This is not ideal over the long term, but is significantly better than regular tap water. You can compromise in the meantime: Filter your water, but add the minerals back in. Purchase good-quality Celtic, Atlantic, Himalayan, or Dead Sea salts. Add just a few grains to your drink bottle and shake well. These natural salts contain many minerals and electrolytes.

Here's a simple observation to make regarding your water quality. Notice how often you need to go to the bathroom after drinking it. After a tall glass, you might need to visit the restroom 30 minutes later. With better-quality water, you may not need to relieve yourself for an hour or more. And, when you *do* go, you'll release less than what you drank—the reason being that your body hasn't simply passed it through. Instead, the water has been used in vital metabolic processes. You're receiving hydration and putting the water you drink to good use.

Measuring your water intake is important, as it helps you get into the routine of adequately hydrating your system. Aim for 0.5 fluid ounces per pound of body weight (30 mL per kilogram) daily. Then, get a water bottle that you can take with you during your daily activities. Please use a glass or stainless-steel bottle. Plastics can leach chemicals and hormonelike substances into water, which, as mentioned earlier, can occur especially in the heat. So, that bottled water in your car should be thrown away and never drunk. If you use glass or stainless steel, you'll be safe. This goes for purchasing water, too. Ideally, buy natural springwater in glass bottles. Or, buy larger home-cooler bottles that are made of hard BPA-free plastic.

Make drinking water fun by adding small amounts of freshly squeezed organic juice, or slices of fresh organic lemon and lime. Combine this with fresh organic mint leaves for a refreshing treat on a warm day.

The angels have guided you to enhance the energy of the water you drink. Now, with every sip, you will be drinking in the vitality and vibration of love.

Full-Moon Blessing

The angels suggest placing water under the light of the full moon, whose energy is intense with manifestation. Doing so will allow you to release all things that you're done with. It welcomes in fresh, new energy for your next phase.

Archangel Gabriel says that it's okay to place glass bottles of water, purchased right from the store, under the moonlight. Perfect—you can gather all the water you'll need for an entire month! Or, just make a special healing batch that you can enjoy for several days. We've found that moon-blessed water tastes sweeter and has a palpable vibration.

Crystal Elixir

Crystals have a healing aura that can infuse liquids. Many healers have worked with this concept by adding stones to their drinking water. Some forms of quartz can be okay, but many minerals and crystals can be harmful in water. For example, malachite can leach out copper, and selenite may dissolve completely. Even when working with quartz, you can't properly eliminate dust and germs. You don't want an elixir of bacteria!

We've been guided to work with the energy of crystals, but the angels have shown us a safe and friendly way to do so. Since crystal energy can pass into water, it can also easily pass through glass. All you need to do is pour yourself a glass of water and then surround the base with healing crystals that you've cleansed. The energies go through the glass and are absorbed into the water. Please do try rose quartz, as it brings a very gentle, calming, and heart-opening energy to your water. The same method works for larger bottles or jugs of water. You'll receive the crystal energy without the fear of unsafe compounds. Do this in the evening before you go to sleep so that you wake up to "crystal elixirs" in the morning.

★ ★ ★

CHAPTER THREE

HERBS AND VITAMINS TO ASSIST YOUR ANGEL DETOX

Herbal medicines are plants that have healing properties. Many parts of the plant may be used, such as the leaves, flowers, fruits, seeds, and roots. Over time, herbalists discovered what the most healing part of each plant was. They also discerned which plants could *not* be taken consumed or taken medicinally.

The story of herbal medicine goes back thousands of years. There are accounts of early humans preserved from the Ice Age clasping bundles of herbs. These same herbs are still used today. That's just one example of the longevity of herbal medicine. If the plants didn't heal, they wouldn't have stood the test of time.

Many herbs were discovered through Divine guidance. Native cultures were very connected to the land and the energies that resided there. As the need for healing arose, village healers would pray for help, and the guidance they received would lead them to particular plants.

Native Americans were guided to echinacea for immune health, although there was no science behind their choice. Pure faith and trust was all they needed. The healing results spoke for themselves. American Indians continued to use echinacea for over 400 years to treat wounds and infections. Word of this miraculous herb soon spread, and herbalists all over the world began using it.

Scientists also heard about this wonderful herb and wanted to learn more. Sadly, when modern research is conducted on herbal medicines, it's often aimed at *dis*proving its effects. However, the scientists couldn't dispute the therapeutic effects of echinacea. They found that there are natural compounds present that trigger your body to produce more white blood cells and aid the activity of other immune cells. This boosts immunity and can help you stay protected from colds and the flu.

Healers are guided to plants and are then instructed on how to use them by God and the angels. As news of their success spreads, others want to know more. Science can help us understand why the plant has a particular healing action, but the next step isn't as helpful. Researchers might then begin animal testing, rationalizing that doing so will help them come up with a "more effective" dosage. They can even remove natural compounds from the herb and use them in isolation. While the materials used are natural, the process can end up being more manufactured.

You can then ask the question: *Who benefits from this?* Is it the patients, as they now take more of the herb? Is it the herbalists, since they now prescribe more medicines? Or, is it the manufacturers, because they're selling a larger turnover of herbal medicines?

Herbs have an energy attached to them, and you can feel their healing properties by holding a bottle of herbal extract or tincture. Please consult with your herbalist or naturopath to see what is right for you. Tell him or her your previous experiences if you've taken herbs before. Also, let this individual know that you're highly sensitive to energy. Be honest with your practitioner. If something is prescribed that doesn't feel right to you, speak up. It's important for you both to share your opinions to achieve an effective healing.

Herbal medicines are available in a variety of forms. Some include liquids such as herbal extracts or tinctures. Others are in the form of tablets, capsules, and teas. Extracts and tinctures are concentrated liquids that usually contain alcohol. Each herb requires a certain percentage of alcohol to extract the therapeutic compounds. Some of these natural chemicals are dissolved in water, and others in alcohol. It's an art to find the perfect balance to get the best of both worlds. This is the research that many herbal companies have already performed. They've discovered which plants are best when extracted in certain percentages of alcohol. The alcohol content should be noted, though, for those with alcohol addictions, or for those people very sensitive to alcohol. For most, extracts and tinctures are an effective way of working with herbs. Your practitioner will combine several herbs to create a magical potion just for you.

Always insist upon organic and non-GMO herbs, vitamins, and minerals. If you're a vegan or vegetarian, check that your supplements don't contain animal products.

The amount of formula you take will depend on the herbs used. It's also dependent on what you're treating. Dosages vary greatly from a few drops to half a fluid ounce (several milliliters). We suggest finding a practitioner who works on a spiritual and energetic level. If your herbalist works in this way, this person will assess your individual requirements and tailor a dosage just for you.

I (Robert) currently find drop doses to be wonderfully effective. They give me flexibility with patients and bring through the profound energy of the plant, too. I feel that each herb has its own personality. This is my current approach to dosage, but I know that it may very well change with the next patient who walks through my door.

So, be sure to trust your own guidance and discuss your concerns with your health-care professional. Allow yourself to be flexible.

Tablets and capsules are easy ways to take herbs and have little or no taste. Make sure that you choose vegetable-derived capsules to avoid gelatin (which is made from cow bones). The tablets and capsules contain powdered raw herb or a powdered liquid extract. There's not much room available in each tablet. So, if it has a raw herb inside, there may not be a very large amount. Other tablets and capsules might say "contains extract equivalent to ___ mg of dried herb." This shows that the product is a dried liquid extract that's more concentrated. Remember, though, that "more concentrated" doesn't equate to being more effective. As products are concentrated, it can lead to some concerns. If the herb being used isn't organic, you may be concentrating pesticides and fertilizers, too.

Herbal teas and healing infusions involve pouring boiling water over the herb and letting it steep. You can use both fresh and dried herbs to make teas. If you have the opportunity to try fresh German chamomile tea, you won't be disappointed. One fresh chamomile flower in a cup of boiling water provides a gentle, yet strong, calming effect. By allowing the herb to sit in water, it sends its vital energies into the liquid. You can then consume the tea and feel the vibrations entering your body.

Add one teaspoon of herb per one cup of boiling water. Teapots are the best option, as trapping in the steam gives you more flavor and more healing benefits. Try a glass teapot for extra enjoyment. Now you can watch your herbs share their magic with the water. Leave the infusion to sit for 10 or 15 minutes prior to drinking. By the way, brewed chamomile tea is a wonderful, chemical-free way to lighten and brighten your hair color if you rinse with it.

Healing Prayer Over Herbs

Before you take your herbal medicine (no matter which form it's in), pay your respects to the plant for its act of service. Take a few moments to infuse your medicine with love and gratitude.

Hold the herb in your hands, or hold your hands just above the herb. Connect to its energy by breathing very deeply. As you relax through this conscious breath, your aura expands. Let your energy mingle with that of the herb. You'll feel a slight pressure, tingling, or warmth in your hands. Next, call upon the healing energy of Archangel Raphael by saying:

"I welcome you, Archangel Raphael, into this space. Please infuse this healing herb with your powerful energy. I thank this herb for its act of service. I ask that this sacred plant heal my physical body, my emotions, and my energy. Please bring me all that I need at this time."

Visualize the herbal medicine glowing with a very bright, white light. Know that this natural medicine will integrate with your body easily and effortlessly. Next, say:

"Angels, I ask you to awaken the spirit of this herb for healing. May your gift of service be well received. Thank you."

Now, allow the herb to do its healing work.

Specific Herbal Medicines for Releasing Toxins

Particular herbs are known for their ability to cleanse. Their action is sometimes called "alterative" or "depurative," which means that they clean the blood. These herbs improve detoxification by assisting in the elimination of waste products, and prevent metabolic toxins from accumulating in the body. Many of them have a long history of treating difficult skin conditions. Perhaps the toxic load became too much for the body to handle, so it began to show an imbalance through the skin.

Barberry (*Berberis vulgaris*) helps heal the stomach and brings strength and tone to the digestive system. This makes it harder for toxins to be absorbed into the bloodstream. It also stimulates the liver and helps the body flush out unwanted chemicals.

Barberry isn't a very pleasant-tasting herb. However, it appears to exert the best healing effect when you taste its bitterness. So, for maximum therapeutic benefit, avoid mixing it with strong-tasting juices, and try water instead.

Blue flag (*Iris versicolor*) releases toxic buildup in the lymphatic system. It helps the all-important lymph, responsible for immunity, to freely circulate. The toxins are then processed through the liver and cleared from the bowel. This herb can also help balance hydration and can work well for chronic skin complaints.

Burdock (*Arctium lappa*) clears toxins from the body by releasing them through the urinary tract. It's effective for relieving aches and pains stemming from gout. It pulls out old toxins and acids that have been stored in the body for some time. These waste products can create skin issues, so by using burdock, you will find that your body cleanses itself and your complexion improves.

Cleavers (*Galium aparine*) is an herb that goes in very deeply— it helps to clear toxins from the intracellular matrix. Many cleansing herbs will remove toxins from the extracellular matrix (the fluid that surrounds your cells). Cleavers removes wastes from inside the cells and helps the body release them. This is something you should approach slowly and gently. If you've never detoxed before, then wait before trying cleavers. If your body is holding on to old metabolic wastes, you may experience symptoms and side effects from your detox.

This herb is extremely cleansing, and you'll feel incredible after using it.

Echinacea (*Echinacea angustifolia* and *Echinacea purpurea*) is possibly one of the most well-known herbs in the world. It stimulates the immune system and sends white blood cells on the hunt for anything harmful. It circulates through the lymphatic system and helps move the flow of toxins out of the body. Then, it repairs any damage they may have caused.

Gotu kola (*Centella asiatica*) is nutritive for the brain. It gently helps circulation reach the top of the head, and breaks down scar tissue, thereby reducing inflammation. Scar tissue can make the body fight harder to achieve balance. By removing unnecessary scar tissue, you can welcome flexibility to your body. Gotu kola also balances the nervous system and brings about clarity of mind. (There are also stories of ancient emperors eating a leaf of gotu kola each day and reaching the age of 200.)

Nettle (*Urtica dioica* or *Urtica urens*) is a very nutritive, detoxifying herb. Its extracts contain vitamins and minerals that promote the production of healthy new blood cells. Nettle clears through the skin, so be sure that you exercise (with a release of perspiration) when taking this herb.

Historically, nettle removed toxins by whipping the bare skin with its stinging leaves. The blisters and rashes that ensued were thought to be toxins and wastes trying to come out. In fact, the needles on the nettle leaf contain histamine, and when touched, they create a rash on the skin. Histamine is responsible for allergic responses, so modern medicine relies heavily on antihistamines to treat allergies. Interestingly, when nettle is taken as a tincture or tea, it *relieves* allergies and hay fever. That's yet another example of the wonders of Mother Nature.

Red clover (*Trifolium pratense*) clears toxins from the body while regulating female hormones. This herb is excellent for the later years in life, both during and after menopause. The irregularity of hormones can lead to changes in mood, energy, and vitality, which can cause you to lose focus and engage in unhealthy habits. Red clover brings about balance where it's needed and ensures that you maintain excellent care of your beautiful body.

Yellow dock (*Rumex crispus*) removes toxins via the bowels. It's a low-dose herb, as higher amounts can cause a laxative effect. Yellow dock is another herb that treats chronic skin complaints, and it also treats toxic bowels. Your body should release toxins from the bowels; if not, they'll be reabsorbed into the bloodstream. This can lead to skin issues that don't respond to regular treatments, so yellow dock will get things moving again!

Herbal Medicines for the Liver

The liver is the primary organ of detoxification. Toxins are processed and metabolized by the liver so they can be safely removed. There are two phases of liver detox. In the initial phase, toxins can become even *more* toxic. They're combined with enzymes that make them water soluble. Often, many environmental toxins are fat soluble, which makes it harder for the body to remove them. Then, in the second phase, they're combined with organic compounds and passed into bile. Your body then releases them through the bowels.

The liver is one of the only human organs that can regenerate. It can regrow to its original size if it's damaged, or partly removed surgically. This is an amazing and loving gift from God. It also shows how immensely important this organ of detox is. Care for your liver to make certain you're able to live a happy, healthy life.

Andrographis (*Andrographis paniculata*) is immune enhancing. It fights infections, especially those of the liver. It protects your precious liver from damage.

Barberry (*Berberis vulgaris*) promotes the production and flow of bile, which assists the body in excreting toxins. In this way, barberry can help detox your body.

Blue flag (*Iris versicolor*) is used when the liver is congested. Associated symptoms can include constipation, nausea, and headaches. Blue flag helps the secretion of bile in order to improve digestion.

Bupleurum (*Bupleurum falcatum*) protects the liver. It reduces inflammation and balances the immune system. It's wonderful for autoimmune conditions that involve the liver.

Dandelion root (*Taraxacum officinale*) stimulates digestion. It triggers the liver to work, and promotes proper bowel function. The grounded energy of dandelion makes it excellent for detox, as it prevents you from losing focus or becoming disheartened.

Sometimes your detox journey may be a long one, so if you persist, you'll be rewarded with wonderful opportunities for health.

Milk thistle, or **St. Mary's thistle** (*Silybum marianum*), is the ultimate liver herb and is beneficial for all aspects of liver function. It encourages this organ to heal and restore itself. It's also highly protective for the liver and prevents damage from drugs and toxins. There have been many studies conducted on milk thistle to prove its protective qualities, several of which have focused on the death-cap mushroom. Milk thistle was able to forestall and delay the damage caused by its poison. Many people take this herb before drinking alcohol, as they find that it's more difficult to get drunk. This herb helps preserve the liver, but this doesn't give you an excuse to drink alcohol to excess.

Rosemary (*Rosmarinus officinalis*) improves memory and concentration. It does so by sending blood to your brain. It also encourages phase II detox from the liver. This is an effective herb to use when detoxing your emotions. It supports your nerves while treating the toxins.

Schizandra, or **shisandra** (*Schisandra chinensis*), nourishes the nerves and balances energy. It helps the liver to perform both phase I and II detoxifications. Use this herb when you're stressed and fatigued but nevertheless need to detox.

Turmeric (*Curcuma longa*) enhances phase I and II detoxifications of the liver. It helps the body clear toxins through bile. It's also an excellent antioxidant and anti-inflammatory. This is a very healing and nutritive herb.

The effects of turmeric can be enhanced if taken with a fat. This might mean mixing the powder with coconut milk, oil, or organic yogurt before ingesting. As a tablet/capsule, it should also be taken with some form of good fat. Perhaps eat a handful of organic almonds, an avocado, or some yogurt.

Liver-Cleansing Dandelion Root Tea

Prepare a healing herbal infusion to stimulate digestion and encourage proper liver function. Dandelion root is a grounding herb that brings awareness back into the body. By drinking a cup or two per day, you can understand what your body wants (food cravings can be confusing if a cause isn't determined). You may crave carbohydrates if you have B-vitamin deficiencies, or crave sugar if you lack magnesium. Your body isn't asking you for carbohydrates in the form of bread and pasta. Instead, it really wants whole grains such as brown rice and legumes like beans. Dandelion tea can help you learn what your body is asking for.

Dandelion root gently stimulates your liver and promotes the removal of wastes. The tea may not be a taste you're familiar with, as it has a very earthy flavor. You can improve the taste by using organic honey, agave syrup, or raw coconut syrup. Avoid adding refined sugar, artificial sweeteners, or milk to your infusion. It may be different from the tea you're used to; however, think of it as medicine. The cup sitting in front of will bring you greater health and offer insights into your body's needs.

Method of Preparation

Add one teaspoon of organic, dried dandelion root (you may also use roasted organic root for a different flavor) to one cup of boiling water. Allow it to steep for ten minutes before tasting, and add natural sweetener if desired.

Elder

Elder is a strong plant that boosts your immunity and protects you from infection. It resonates with the upper respiratory system, meaning the nose, throat, and sinuses.

Even the healthiest of us can be prone to a runny nose. Elder is a good friend to have on hand in such a case. I (Robert) have worked with it countless times and have found that after just a day or two of using it, a runny nose goes away completely.

Elder has a long history, both in traditional herbal medicine and folklore. Every plant has an energy or spirit contained within it. If you sit quietly with a plant, you'll soon come to learn more about it. Plants are so willing to share their healing and knowledge with you. This kind of thinking may be considered on the more spiritual and esoteric side. However, the "Elder Mother" is known by spiritualists and the lay farmer alike, and there are ancient stories that forbid the burning of elder wood. To this day, some farmers and country folk refuse to harm her. They know that she needs her space and that they should give her the care and attention she deserves. After all, they want to benefit from her healing properties when the time arises.

Elder has a "louder" personality than most. When connecting to her, you'll be met by a warm and caring energy. Elder certainly wants to help with your healing, yet she demands respect. It's a two-way street. If you want her medicine, then you have to treat her well in return. This is fine if you're living in a rural setting and grow elder trees, yet most of us are buying elderflowers or berries already harvested and prepared commercially.

So what can you do to ensure a good result and keep the Elder Mother on your side? Sit down with your bottle and close your eyes. Silently ask for healing help from elder. You might like to offer something back to the earth in return. Consider leaving a treat outside, or pouring some juice onto the grass. Provided your intentions are pure, you'll get along wonderfully! It's important to listen to elder after taking the medicine. Often you'll be guided to get more rest, so give yourself more care and allow for a "time-out." This is an important aspect of your healing, so please acknowledge and indulge it.

Elderflowers come from the *Sambucus nigra* tree. These tiny white flowers are cultivated as an herbal medicine for colds, fevers, and runny noses and are very effective and safe. They come in a number of preparations, including tea, herbal extracts, tinctures, and tablets. Taking eight drops of tincture three to four times a day is all that's needed.

Elderberries are making a comeback, and research is showing that they have powerful antiviral properties, which makes them wonderfully effective for flu symptoms. Modern medicine lacks the ability to treat viral infections, so when you're given antibiotics for the flu, this doesn't treat the virus. Instead, your doctor is preventing you from getting a secondary infection caused by bacteria. By using elderberries, you can boost your body's ability to fight off a virus.

The issue with elderberries is that they're unstable as a fluid. Most herbs are extracted into a liquid and then taken as such, or dried into a powder. Due to the temperamental nature of these berries, other methods have to be employed. Tablets are most effective.

Taking elderflowers as a tea can help break fevers, which must be monitored closely. Ensure that they never get too high (close to 104°F/40°C). If they do, seek medical help immediately. Otherwise, add two teaspoons of dried elderflowers to a cup of boiling water. Infuse for ten minutes, strain, and then drink. This warm drink helps to fight illness and normalize body temperature. It almost sounds like the opposite of what you should do. However, by drinking warm fluids, you're more likely to induce sweating. Once the fever "breaks into a sweat," the temperature should drop and healing will occur. It's a great idea to drink elderflower tea during the cooler months as a preventive method as well. You might also like to try the popular yarrow, elderflower, and peppermint combination.

Echinacea

Echinacea is possibly the most famous herbal medicine. It has a long tradition of success, yet there is still debate over its effectiveness. You may have tried echinacea and not had good results, so we want to share the best times to take this wonderful herb, and also how to find a good product.

Echinacea is an immune-boosting herb. It helps restore your immune function and increase the white blood cells in your system, which protects you from infections. However, if you've already succumbed to a cold or illness, then echinacea may not be the herb for you. It's best taken for two or three months to help strengthen your immunity. If you get ill, don't decide to start taking echinacea then, as it's too late. It will still help, but will not be as effective as herbs such as garlic or andrographis, which are excellent for acute illness. Echinacea is better suited to a long-term plan for improved health and well-being.

Make sure you choose a product that uses the most beneficial species of herb. *Echinacea angustifolia* and *echinacea purpurea* are the best forms you can find. They are both highly effective, and wonderful for your immune system. *Echinacea pallida* is often used in lesser-quality products. This species doesn't possess the same immune-boosting power as the other forms, but manufacturers will use it because it's less expensive and they can still put "echinacea" on the label. Check the ingredients list on every product, and make sure you're getting the best quality.

The most effective part of echinacea is the root, as it contains the highest concentration of active compounds. However, we like products that use the whole plant: root, leaves, and flowers. This means that nothing is wasted. If we're pulling the herb from the ground and asking it to be of service, the least we can do is use it in its entirety. Don't disrespect Mother Nature by using only the root and throwing the rest away.

Cordyceps

Cordyceps (*Cordyceps sinensis*) is a tonic herb that builds immunity, vitality, and physical endurance. It was a little-known substance until 1992 when the Chinese Olympians broke records in multiple events. They were tested (like all other athletes) for drugs, but everything came back clear. It was then found that these elite athletes were consuming cordyceps as part of their daily regime. Cordyceps may enhance the uptake of oxygen by the cells, which serves to benefit every area of your body. As oxygen is exchanged, you release carbon dioxide and other metabolic wastes. This allows you to work at a higher intensity without fatigue.

Cordyceps balances your immune system and is perfect for long-term complaints. It strengthens your body after a long illness, surgery, or other occasions that are both physically and emotionally draining. This powerful herb grows at high altitudes in the mountains of China and Tibet and withstands harsh environments and cold winters, which shows its adaptability. This miraculous herb brings those same virtues to *you,* giving you the stamina to complete your tasks.

Cordyceps has been used to treat coughs, respiratory concerns, low libido, cardiovascular issues, and weakness. It is a tonic that promotes a long life, improves energy levels, and increases stamina. It also increases the body's natural killer cells, which destroy unhealthy cells. Some studies have found that it's beneficial to use cordyceps along with chemotherapy treatments. This is best discussed with the treating specialist.

Healing Flowers to Release Addictions

Every flower contains magical healing properties. However, there are a few that stand out when it comes to releasing addictions. These are agapanthus, iris, and white magnolia. Being addicted to something can simply mean that you crave it; it doesn't have to involve an illicit drug or some other type of harmful substance. People can become addicted to almost anything.

Judging yourself for what you may be addicted to serves no benefit. Call upon your loving angels for guidance. They'll ask you to find supportive helpers who cherish you and want to see you succeed. Choose loving friends and family members you can share your health goals with. These people will monitor your progress and also help you stay on track. When releasing addictive behaviors, you need to be around people who hold you accountable, so find those who have your best interests at heart.

Agapanthus clears the energy of deeply ingrained issues, leaving nothing behind. This is perfect for addictions, as they often spill over into many areas of your life. By working with agapanthus, you can balance all these areas at once. It's especially useful when other people's energies are a problem. If you have friends or family members who encourage or enable your addictions, you'll find comfort and support with agapanthus.

Iris deals with the energy of detoxification. This healing flower guides you to release all that no longer serves you. This includes foods, drinks, habits, and all types of relationships. Iris brings to your attention those symptoms that your habits are creating. It illuminates the true cause of your current state of health. As you work with iris, your vitality will rise. Connect to your spark of life and develop newfound motivation. You'll start performing tasks you've put off for a long time, or you'll restart things that you've missed doing in the past.

White magnolias have giant flowers. They're superb at clearing negative energies and toxins from your environment, and dissolve negative effects of electromagnetic radiation. These flowers increase your sensitivity, and the more sensitive you become, the more you "feel" within your being. This is a very powerful and useful tool to have as a lightworker. It helps you identify which foods, drinks, or environments are too harsh for you.

The angels guide you to avoid situations causing you pain and stress, so allow them to help you smoothly transition to a space that contains only love. Trust in the guidance you receive, as God and the angels always urge you to aspire to your highest good.

Vitamin C

Vitamin C is needed for so much more than immune support. It also repairs the skin, restores energy, fights infection, and is a powerful antioxidant. This important nutrient is water soluble, meaning that your body doesn't have reserves of it, like it does with iron. So, a constant supply needs to go into your body through what you eat. Foods rich in vitamin C are the ones that are brightly colored, such as oranges, lemons, limes, strawberries, blueberries, bell peppers, and so on.

Enjoy these foods as part of your daily diet, but remember that it's very important to source local, organic produce. Every second that the fruit is off the tree, it's losing nutrition. Does anyone really know how long that produce in the supermarket has been sitting there? For all you know, it was picked months ago, stored in a freezer, and transported all over the country. However, if you can find a local, organic farmer, you can enjoy really fresh, nutritious foods. Better still, you can plant your own organic garden!

It's a good idea to take vitamin C supplements occasionally to ensure that you're getting enough. When using vitamin C, make sure it's derived from organic corn or other organic sources. Commercial vitamin C is usually made from nonorganic corn, which means that it contains bug poison. When looking for supplements, choose those that have multiple sources of vitamin C, not just ascorbic acid. Make sure there are other mineral ascorbates present, such as sodium ascorbate, calcium ascorbate, and so on. The additional ascorbates buffer the acid and create a gentler effect internally. Taking too much isolated ascorbic acid may lead to stomach pains and unexpected trips to the bathroom.

Once you've found a balanced supplement, check the quantity of vitamin C per dose. Powders, tablets, and capsules are all fine, provided that there aren't extra ingredients in your chosen product. Check with your physician or naturopath to determine the maximum dose best suited for you, which could be up to 2,000 milligrams per day.

Vitamin C is well known for its ability to boost the immune system. It's antibiotic and antiviral. When taken at the onset of a cold or flu, this vitamin can reduce the severity and duration of the infection. Take small doses of vitamin C more frequently to enhance your immune function. In this case, larger doses won't help. Rather, your body needs a constant supply of small, manageable doses that it can readily absorb and utilize.

Vitamin C works with your white blood cells, and when they're balanced, your body becomes a well-structured and protected vessel. Your white blood cells constantly circulate, checking for any signs of infection or illness. At the first sighting, they're sent to work to destroy harmful cells.

Vitamin C is also an excellent healer for the skin. It promotes collagen synthesis and brings tissues together in a harmonious way. You can purchase vitamin C lotions for topical treatment on the face. These are luxurious, nurturing products that your skin readily drinks up. Your skin will glow with vitality and health when you apply natural, chemical-free products to it. Since vitamin C has such an affinity for the skin already, the topical lotions get to work right away. Remember, also, that the skin is one of the largest organs for detoxification. If your skin is clogged and congested by toxins, you can't release the nasty chemicals. When you have high levels of vitamin C in your system, you'll have radiant skin; and you'll also notice that when you exercise, your body easily sweats. This is a natural process of removing unwanted waste. You'll probably find that your sweat has little or no odor compared with others'—this is because your body has flushed out the toxins and has left you cleansed.

The healing properties of vitamin C also include repairing your precious adrenal glands, restoring your natural energy levels, and rebuilding any damage caused by chronic stress. Your adrenal glands are an energy powerhouse responsible for creating adrenaline—the heart-pumping, energizing compound that enlivens you. Adrenaline can be released when you're excited and motivated. Unfortunately, during stress adrenaline is being released all too often. If your body has to cope with the demands of stress for lengthy periods of time, it becomes weak. You start to lose strength in your adrenal glands and head toward adrenal exhaustion. Vitamin C searches your body for any free radicals and neutralizes them, protecting you from their damaging effects. This antioxidant quality has made vitamin C a key vitamin in anti-aging treatments. It prevents cellular damage and enhances the youthfulness of your cells.

Vitamin D

Vitamin D deficiency is becoming more and more common. As we spend countless hours indoors under artificial lighting, and as sunlight is obliterated by environmental pollutants, we become deficient in vitamin D. This is the nutrient you absorb from sunlight, which is so healing and soothing and brings you other needed vitamins, too!

You need unfiltered light to absorb vitamin D, so sitting next to a window or driving a car doesn't count, because the glass blocks the ultraviolet rays that stimulate vitamin D synthesis. Covering yourself in sunscreen blocks the pathway to vitamin D, too. Of course, you must be mindful of exposure to the sun, and if your skin isn't used to being outdoors, you'll likely burn. Sunburn isn't beneficial for anyone, so gently and carefully introduce yourself to sunlight. Early-morning and late-afternoon sunshine is perfect for getting your vitamin D. Research suggests that you only need 15 minutes of uninterrupted sunshine to get all your vitamin D for the day. Sadly, many people don't even spend this short amount of time outdoors.

People in the corporate world often wear suits and long sleeves, covering their bodies from the sun. The artificial lighting in offices (and many homes) is dangerous to the health, too, as fluorescent lighting can suppress the secretion of melatonin. Melatonin works with your sleep cycle and balances your mood. It tells you when you're tired and when to wake up. After long-term exposure to fluorescent lighting, the brain becomes confused. The messages get damaged, and your sleep cycles start to suffer. Subsequently, your mood deteriorates, and concentration soon starts to drop. Yes, these lights are publicized as being energy efficient; however, they contain mercury. If one of these bulbs breaks, it's advised that you evacuate the area. Do you really want something this dangerous hanging above your head all day? Compact fluorescent lights are a smaller version of the traditional long-tube lights. These are typically coiled, or can look like regular bulbs. Be sure to read packaging to find out information about the bulb you're about to buy.

Fluorescent lights also create "dirty electricity," which is electromagnetic radiation that's difficult for your body to process. "Clean electricity" produces very little electromagnetic radiation, as the waves of electricity are consistent. However, dirty electricity has peaks and valleys that alter your nervous system. Being exposed to fluorescent lights can have an almost immediate effect on you. Experiments have been done on diabetic patients where first their blood sugar was regulated, and then they were placed in an area filled with dirty electricity. Their blood-sugar levels rose significantly. As soon as they were taken away from this "dirty" environment, their blood sugar came back into balance.

The angels say that these chemical-laden lights are damaging to our intuition; and that the waves of energy coming from the bulbs block our ability to clearly hear, see, feel, and know them (the angels). You may have noticed that it's more difficult to receive messages from these Heavenly beings in shopping centers or office buildings. But as soon as you leave such areas, suddenly you have a different perspective on a recent purchase or commitment. This is because you've removed yourself from the harsh electromagnetic radiation associated with fluorescent lights. Now you can connect with your angels again!

Being so sensitive, you may notice headaches, tiredness, and a lack of focus when you're in those environments. Additionally, anyone wanting to do healing work or give readings should avoid fluorescent lighting in their offices. Many healers will intuitively feel this and switch off the overhead lights and opt for gentle lamps instead.

Old-style lightbulbs (incandescents) are much better for your health, but they're not very energy efficient. The new halogen bulbs produce great light, too, but again, are not the most energy-efficient options. LED lights, in contrast, are excellent indoor lighting options, as they're energy efficient, produce little electromagnetic radiation, and emit bright light.

Vitamin D is absorbed from the sun, although some may find it helpful to supplement, too. Vitamin D is fat soluble. This means that as your body absorbs it, it can get stored in fat cells and circulate through fluid. The beauty of this is that you can raise your levels quite quickly, and then your body retains this valuable nutrient.

Choose a good-quality supplement in the form of cholecalciferol. This is vitamin D_3 and is readily absorbed by the body. Since vitamin D is fat soluble, many supplements add a fat, like olive oil, to the product. This helps with absorption and the stability of the nutrient. Some higher-quality supplements are refrigerated, as they contain pure vitamin D_3.

Testing of your vitamin D levels can be easily performed by your doctor. A blood test will show your current levels and then help you assess how much of the vitamin you need to supplement with. Or, it can help you realize the importance of going outdoors.

A general dosage for vitamin D is 1,000 IU per day. Take it with food, and ideally with a fat. Consider taking a teaspoon of coconut oil just before your vitamin D. If you're very deficient, you may need more. This is best talked over with your naturopath.

For many years, vitamin D was only known to strengthen bones, giving them more density, along with calcium. In recent years, vitamin D has been extensively researched. Now we find that it's responsible for several immune-system functions. The Westmead Children's Hospital in Australia is currently looking at the effectiveness of using vitamin D for the treatment of eczema and dermatitis. It also appears to have a hormonal action.

Vitamin D is responsible for the maintenance of cells, and could be an important factor in treating many cancers and auto-immune conditions. All in all, having enough vitamin D in your system may protect you against numerous health issues.

Fiber

Fiber is a component of food that is essential to your good health. There is soluble and insoluble fiber, and you need both for a fully functioning digestive system. The angels have revealed that fiber has a life force of its own. In your body, it aids your digestion and promotes greater health in two ways: (1) clearing away toxins, and (2) feeding the beneficial bacteria in your digestive system.

Soluble fiber is found in fresh fruits, vegetables, legumes, beans, oats, and rice. It attracts water and can make you feel fuller, longer. It helps lower blood pressure and may balance blood-sugar levels. It also delays the absorption of sugar, thereby preventing blood-sugar spikes.

Insoluble fiber is found in cereals and whole grains like brown rice. It has a bulking effect within your digestive system that keeps you regular. Insoluble fibers also include psyllium husks, bran, and slippery elm powder. This fiber remains totally unchanged during its journey through the body.

By including plenty of fiber in your diet, you'll discover that your body naturally cleanses itself of waste products. Fiber prevents you from holding on to toxic compounds and helps you remove them. Harmful toxins can stick to the lining of your bowel, and as they sit there, they become more toxic and dangerous. You need to eliminate them from your bowel in a safe and natural way. Think of fiber like a pipe cleaner: it cleans away any internal debris that can cause ill health. The fiber attaches to cholesterol and chemicals and carries them out of your body.

Fiber serves as a *prebiotic,* which is the source of nourishment to your digestive system's healthy bacteria. To colonize your bowels with healthy organisms, the bacteria need something to feed off, so fiber is the answer. People will too often take a probiotic supplement and achieve little benefit. If they include this treatment plan with adequate fiber, their results will certainly improve.

If you opt for a fiber supplement, avoid taking it with other medications and supplements. Elements in the fiber can bind with the helpful compounds in your supplement and prevent it from being absorbed. Also, make sure you drink plenty of water before taking a fiber supplement, and an *additional* glass of water at the time you're taking it. If you don't, then the insoluble fiber may swell and block your bowels. By consuming enough water with the fiber, the cleansing process will occur as nature intended.

★ ★ ★

CHAPTER FOUR

Aromatherapy and Essential Oils

One easy way to detox your body and home is to switch from chemical-laden toiletries and cleaning supplies to natural essential oils. You'll save money and help the environment, too!

Pure essential oils are concentrated healing remedies that come from plants. Almost all plants have essential oils within them. The price will depend on how abundant they are and how easily they can be extracted. For example, lemon and orange essential oil is concentrated in the peel of these citrus fruits. The oil willingly comes out, making a pure, aromatic, yet very affordable oil.

On the other hand, true rose oil comes from the petals, which are very lightweight. It takes up to 1,000 petals to make even one drop of oil, which makes pure 100 percent rose oil extremely expensive. It will usually be diluted with odorless jojoba oil as a carrier. This is fine, as the Heavenly scent still emanates from this sacred oil.

Each oil has its own unique scent, vibration, and healing properties. The angels are always around when you work with essential oils, and their aromas tend to open up your psychic abilities by heightening your intuition. The fragrance of the oils transcends the physical world and awakens your spiritual body. They detox you physically, emotionally, and psychically.

A Selection of Essential Oils and Chakras

Chakra	Essential Oils
Root	Patchouli
Sacral	Jasmine, sandalwood
Solar plexus	Vetiver, geranium, fennel, juniper
Heart	Bergamot, rose
Throat	Blue chamomile, palmarosa
Third Eye	Rosemary
Ear	Lavender, peppermint
Crown	Frankincense, neroli

Healing Properties and Associated Angels for Some Essential Oils

Cedarwood

Cedarwood has an earthy aroma that ties you to your heritage and helps bring you back to your roots. Cedarwood links you with your heritage by grounding your energy. It is connected with Archangel Jeremiel.

Chamomile

Chamomile is wonderfully calming and relaxing. It relieves stress and anxieties of all kinds. Chamomile is anti-inflammatory and can soothe red, inflamed skin conditions.

This beautiful blue oil resonates with the throat chakra. Chamomile balances your communication and enhances your voice. It gives you confidence when making speeches and allows you to write more effectively. Sharing messages with others is healing to both parties—those giving and those receiving. This oil helps you to get your point across in a gentle and loving way. Work with chamomile if you feel you have something to say but can't find the audience yet. It is connected to Archangels Gabriel and Michael.

Clove

Clove oil cleans mold and prevents it from returning. Many products for cleaning mold contain toxic chemicals that are dangerous to breathe in and live around. Clove helps remove the mold and stops the spores from spreading. Use the oil undiluted, and wipe over the affected areas. Always try a small test patch to make sure the oil doesn't stain walls. You can also use clove oil in your aromatherapy diffuser to clear mold spores from the air.

Clove instantly removes any feelings of "spaciness." It brings you back into the moment and plants your feet on the ground. This is a wonderful oil to use after a deep healing or meditation. It's quite strong, so only a small amount is needed. It can be helpful during spiritual events, as it keeps you in your body. It is connected to Archangels Azrael, Metatron, and Zadkiel.

Eucalyptus

Eucalyptus cleanses the air of bacteria and viruses, and is a great antiseptic oil that will protect you during the winter months. It lifts tension from the chest and heals coughs and respiratory congestion. Place a few drops of eucalyptus oil on a tissue and inhale it throughout the day to soothe nasal congestion.

This oil is deeply cleansing, both physically and spiritually. It clears the energy of psychic attacks and unwanted spirits. Eucalyptus can bring up old energies and emotions in order to release them. This step is important in your healing. Sometimes it's imperative that you acknowledge the past so that you can move into a brighter future. It is connected to Archangels Michael and Raphael.

Frankincense

Frankincense is beneficial for the skin and has been used for anti-aging and skin healing. Try adding one or two drops to half a teaspoon of carrier oil (jojoba, olive, or coconut) and gently massage into the skin. After a week, you'll notice an improved glow in your complexion.

The sacred aroma of frankincense allows you to connect to God and the angels more easily. It brings through ancient wisdom that your soul already understands. If you're a teacher, this oil will help you educate others about spirituality. As you work with frankincense, you'll gain deeper spiritual understanding. It is strongly connected to Archangel Raziel, the Angel of Spiritual Teachers.

Geranium

Geranium can be helpful when traveling. It regulates your body clock and balances your sleep/waking cycles. It's calming and uplifting all at the same time. This oil also enhances your self-esteem and confidence. It is connected to Archangels Haniel and Jophiel.

Juniper

Only a small amount of this oil is needed to remove anything that no longer serves you. It helps you realize when it's time to release people, things, and situations; and clears away unwanted thoughts and burdens. Juniper is excellent protection against harsh, prickly people. Keep it in your office or home to safeguard you against negative individuals. It is connected to Archangels Metatron and Michael.

Lavender

Lavender is antiseptic and a great cleaning oil. Use it in a spray for tabletops, or in water to mop the floor. It kills germs and leaves a beautiful fragrance throughout the home.

Lavender oil is the ultimate oil for relaxation. A simple inhalation of this aroma instantly clears your mind and creates tranquility.

A thought is a very powerful tool for manifestation. Whatever you focus your intention on is what you'll receive in the physical world. Focus on calm, relaxing, and peaceful thoughts, and this is what you will experience in the physical world when working with this oil. All stress and drama will leave your life as you embrace the positive field surrounding you. Lavender opens your third-eye chakra and awakens your natural clairvoyant abilities. It is connected with Archangel Haniel.

Lemon

This oil is a natural disinfectant. Place a few drops on nonporous surfaces, and wipe. The lemon oil will cleanse the area of any bacteria or other germs. Or, you can combine this with tea tree oil in a cleaning spray.

Lemon oil dissolves heavier energies and releases negative patterns from your life. It is connected with Archangels Metatron and Raguel.

Orange

This oil brings balance to your life and helps you focus more clearly on your goals. It enhances your self-confidence, and motivates you to achieve your desires. Before you attain your goals, you have to know what they are first. Orange oil brings greater clarity to your desires and aspirations. By working with this oil, you'll understand what makes you truly passionate and see how to enjoy these passions every single day. It is connected with Archangels Chamuel, Sandalphon, and Uriel.

Patchouli

Patchouli is grounding and brings you back into your body. It helps get you out of your head and into your heart. (All your thoughts and focus should come from a heart-centered space.) When you work with patchouli oil, you'll feel more stable and balanced. It is connected with Archangels Metatron and Zadkiel.

Peppermint

Peppermint is excellent for relieving pain. Apply a single drop to your temples if you have a headache; rub a drop or two on your abdomen for menstrual pain. Basically, apply anywhere there's discomfort or inflammation. Using the oil straight will cause some slight redness on the skin, as it will bring blood to the surface to promote healing. If you like, you can mix it with a little carrier oil to dilute it.

Peppermint balances your moods—it's an uplifting oil that builds motivation. It is connected to Archangel Raphael.

Rose

Rose oil is a signature scent for love. It immediately brings you to a heart-centered space, with your total awareness being focused on love, which is the ultimate healer. Everything that comes from a place of love is healing; and all healing encompasses love. Therefore, the more love you surround yourself with, the more healing energy you'll experience. Rose oil brings you peace and tranquility through its delicate aroma. It is connected with Archangels Haniel, Jophiel, and Raphael.

Rosemary

Rosemary oil has an affinity for the head area. It penetrates mental fogs and boosts concentration. It allows you to focus, as well as gain greater understanding of the tasks at hand. It awakens your third eye and brings through your intuitive guidance. Rosemary enhances your spiritual abilities by giving you greater clarity. It is connected with Archangels Michael, Raziel, and Uriel.

Sandalwood

This sacred oil has an allure that invokes high spiritual wisdom and knowledge. It passes on the secrets of the Universe to you, and unlocks the mysteries held within. It can be an excellent oil to use when working with clients, as you'll reach new depths of insight and uncover the true source of their concerns. Sandalwood balances your physical and mental desires, enhancing your creativity and helping you be comfortable with who you are. It is connected with Archangels Michael, Raziel, and Uriel.

Tea Tree

Tea tree oil is a natural disinfectant that can be used for cleaning all areas of your home. The fresh scent leaves your home smelling cleaner, too! Tea tree is one of the only oils that can break through the biofilm of bacteria. When bacteria group together on surfaces, they secrete a film that protects them. Tea tree oil can break this shield down and remove the bacteria entirely. Also, studies have shown that bacteria are unable to form a resistance to this magical oil.

Tea tree oil breaks down old, stagnant energy to make room for the new. It helps with growth and adaptation to your current situation. It unblocks your chakras by dissolving negative energy, and is connected with Archangels Michael and Raphael.

Hand Spray

To keep yourself and your family healthy, cleaning your hands is essential. As you go about your day running errands, you'll come into contact with a multitude of germs. Think of shopping carts, door handles, restroom surfaces, and handrails as hot spots for germs.

Hand sanitizers are filled with harsh chemicals and toxins such as triclosan, so these products should be avoided! However, there are natural hand sanitizers that are made from botanical cleansers. Read the labels carefully, though, as many will still contain artificial and synthetic fragrances and chemicals.

After doing some research, we've decided that it's safest and easiest for us to make our own. Add 200 drops (roughly two teaspoons) of tea tree essential oil to a 3 fl. oz./100 mL bottle filled with water. Shake it vigorously to incorporate the oils. You can make your spray more effective by adding an emulsifying agent. Many quality essential-oil suppliers will have something you can mix with the oils to make them blend with water. Make sure they're from natural, nonallergenic sources. Carry this spray (or decant into smaller bottles), and spray your hands (or applicable surfaces) as you need to. The natural antiseptic property of tea tree oil will remove any bacteria.

Natural Deodorant

Most essential oils are antibacterial in nature. It's bacteria that cause body odor and discomfort. Conventional deodorants aim to prevent bacteria from forming and also inhibit perspiration. They do this through the inclusion of harmful and toxic substances such as aluminum, which will negatively impact your brain. Studies have shown a direct correlation between aluminum exposure and dementia.

You can make your own deodorant using a method similar to that of hand spray. Simply change the oils to your liking. You might find that you don't need as high a ratio of oil to water.

Experiment with your body by starting off slow and building up to a higher concentration if needed. Lavender is a good staple, as it's antibacterial and antifungal. Combine this with some rose or chamomile oil for a beautiful, natural fragrance. Mist under your arms and allow to air-dry. Only a few sprays are needed.

Or, you can apply the oil directly to your underarms. Rub in a few drops of lavender oil for all-day freshness.

Body Oil

Create a healing and detoxifying body oil for yourself. You can choose the essential oils that go in it through your intuition. The base of the oil should be natural and chemical-free. Use organic jojoba oil, organic extra-virgin cold-pressed olive oil, or organic extra-virgin coconut oil. All of these will take to essential oils readily and easily.

Start with 1 fl. oz./30 mL and add up to 15 drops of essential oil. Follow your guidance with this, and meditate on the blend before you make it. For example, you may be guided to use 1 drop of rose and 14 drops of lavender. Let the angels help you with this formula.

Once combined, rub a few drops on your chest, arms, and legs. It's enlivening to start the day in this fashion. Your senses (including your psychic sense) come alive! Using essential oils as part of massage therapy is a beautiful way to detox.

★ ★ ★

CHAPTER FIVE

DETOXING YOUR KITCHEN

The father of modern medicine, Hippocrates, said: "Let food be thy medicine, and medicine be thy food." The foods you eat have a huge effect on your energy levels, ability to focus, moods, appearance, and health.

As we emphasized earlier in this book, there's a disturbing rise in genetically modified foods hitting our store shelves. GM foods have had their genetic structures manipulated; often, the reasons for doing so are to prolong shelf life and increase resilience to insects. Some GM foods, such as corn, actually have insect-killing poisons built inside of them. So you're consuming a toxin when you eat or drink a genetically modified corn product. The manufacturers suggest that the food is virtually the same as organic food; however, some studies show that genetically engineered foods lead to sterility and tumors in lab animals. So why take a chance with your health when organic non-GM food tastes better and is risk-free?

Labeling and disclosure laws are different in every country. Currently in the United States, there are GM foods on most store shelves. They hide in many packaged products, too, and go unlabeled and unnamed. In Australia and parts of Europe, the product must state it contains GM sources.

Your safest option is to choose certified organic products. By doing so, you can feel confident that the food you consume is natural and whole, as God intended.

Common Genetically Modified Foods to Avoid

Potatoes

Corn (including corn syrup, corn powder)

Beets (including beet sugar)

Rice

Soy products (including soybean oil)

Squash

Wheat

Hawaiian papayas

Tomatoes

Yeast

Bananas

Honey (bees feed off GMO canola, and most honey is adulterated with GMO corn syrup)

Salmon

Aspartame (NutraSweet)

Cottonseed oil

Canola/rapeseed oil

Peas

Meat, eggs, and dairy products
(cows and chickens are fed GMO feed and are given growth hormones, antibiotics, and other additives that enter their milk and flesh; in addition, if an animal suffered during its life or slaughter, the by-products are filled with pain energy, which transfers to whoever consumes these items)

The Concept of a Rotational Diet

Your body does best when you rotate your foods. This means that if you eat organic tomatoes today, avoid them for several days before enjoying them again. This applies to all foods and drinks. Your body is sensitive, as you know, so if you overconsume the same foods or drinks each and every day, you create inflammation—you no longer recognize the foods as sources of nutrition. Rather, your body sets up an inflammatory process that prevents you from absorbing nourishment.

Interestingly, you can become addicted to the foods you're allergic to. As your body creates inflammation, it releases endorphins, which are the feel-good hormones that you become addicted to. So, you eat the tomato (or whatever food you overconsume), which makes you feel good. At the same time, your body creates inflammation. Your mind makes the connection with feeling good after eating this food, so you eat more of it, releasing more endorphins.

Until you stop and process this experience, you won't realize that your body is lacking the nourishment it requires. So consider avoiding the food you overindulge in for several weeks. Notice the subtle and profound differences within your body. Then, you can try the food again to see how your body reacts. This time you might find that you feel bloated, tired, itchy, or uncomfortable when you eat the food. This is a clear sign that the food was never your friend. You'll get to the point where you can enjoy these foods again. However, you must do some work on your digestive system.

First, plan your meals. It will take some time and effort to do so, but you'll be glad you did. Sit down one weekend and plan out the next week's meals. Include breakfast, a morning snack, lunch, an afternoon snack, and dinner. By writing this down, you'll avoid eating food impulsively. You can monitor your consumption, too. As you get into the routine of doing so, prepare more weekly plans. Aim to create three or four weeks' worth that feature different meals. You'll be able to enjoy a wide variety of foods with few bodily complaints. You'll also know what you need to purchase. This cuts down on food waste and reduces your shopping bill.

A woman named Rachel Marshall told us that she'd always been vegetarian but was guided to become vegan over the last five years. Rachel received the message to eat raw food during the month of November. She affectionately called it "Rawvember." By being fed high-energy, living food, her body detoxed itself, releasing old emotions and pain from the past. As she began eating in a more balanced way, she felt lighter and more alive!

Safe and Unsafe Cookware

Being serious about detox means that you're willing to limit your exposure to toxins. This includes your cooking. Not only should you be mindful of the quality of food you prepare, but you should also take into account the pan in which it's cooked.

Let's look at unsafe cookware first.

Aluminum: Aluminum is a highly toxic way to cook. This dangerous metal has been linked to Alzheimer's disease and dementia. The aluminum is stored in the brain and affects its capabilities. It heats very quickly, which is why it's often used in cookware. However, when heated, it leaches into food very easily—even more so if it's used to cook acidic foods. Some companies are using aluminum as the core of their cookware. It is surrounded with a safer material and still gives you great heating. If the surface becomes damaged, though, your food could be exposed to the aluminum, so it's safest to avoid cooking with any product that contains traces of this metal.

Teflon: Teflon pots and pans are very popular, as this substance prevents foods from sticking. It's very easy to scratch the surface of these pans and damage the Teflon coating, which may cause small traces to enter your food, which you can accidentally ingest. Also, scratching the surface of the pot or pan exposes the metal underneath, which is very likely a harmful metal such as aluminum. When heated, Teflon releases toxic fumes into the air, which you breathe in and absorb into your system. We recommend avoiding Teflon-coated and nonstick pans.

Plastic: Plastic shouldn't even be an option for cooking. When heated or microwaved, it releases toxic chemicals into food that create health issues. Most plastics will leach xenoestrogens or BPA when heated. These artificial hormones sit on your natural estrogen receptors and cause hormonal imbalances. So never heat a plastic container or add hot foods or liquids to a plastic bowl.

If you're storing leftovers in plastic containers, always choose the BPA-free variety. You can find more about this topic online.

★

Now let's look at some safer ways to cook:

Stainless steel: Some sources say that stainless steel cookware is safe; others say that if it's used to cook acidic foods, it can leach nickel, cobalt, and chromium into your food. To make steel stainless, nickel needs to be present. This is a metal that can cause allergies in sensitive individuals. Many chefs will search for the highest percentage of nickel in steel cookware because these items will be the shiniest, and purportedly be the "best" quality. But in actuality, less nickel is better for your health. A simple technique to test for nickel is to take a magnet with you to the store. The more magnetic the pan, the less nickel is present.

Ceramic: Ceramic cookware is safe to use. The only caution is if the glaze contains lead or other toxins. Ceramic-enameled cast-iron cookware can be quite safe. It offers versatility, as it can go from the stove to the oven, and provides a more nonstick surface. Be gentle when cleaning this product to avoid chipping or scratching the ceramic.

Glass: Glass cookware is safe, too. Use modern, recently made glass pots to avoid possible lead exposure. Heating glassware requires practice, as it's not as good at conducting heat as ceramic and steel. Never run a hot glass dish under cold water—this could cause it to crack and break. Glass cookware is temperature tested and will indicate how it can be used—that is, in the oven, on the stovetop, and so on. Follow manufacturer guidelines and avoid misusing these products. You can bake a beautiful meal in this type of cookware and have the pleasure of seeing it through the glass.

Cast iron: Your grandmother probably cooked with an iron skillet. Iron cookware requires "seasoning," which means baking the cookware with oil to create a nonstick surface. Once the iron-ware is properly seasoned, it creates a uniform heating surface, and some of the iron that leaches into the food can be healthful. However, too much iron can lead to fatigue in men and menopausal women, so if you fall into these categories, then use cast iron sparingly.

Clay: Clay cookware is an ancient way to cook. The unglazed clay seals in nutrients, similar to steaming.

Bamboo: Bamboo steamers are my (Doreen's) favorite way to cook. You can buy bamboo steamers online, at cooking stores, and at many health-food stores. These steamers have separated levels that allow you to put the denser foods (such as broccoli and carrots) nearer to the boiling water, and more delicate foods (such as spinach) farther away from the heat. This way, everything cooks at once. Bamboo steamers are a nontoxic way to cook without fats or oils.

Nontoxic Kitchen Cleaners

Most people keep their cleaning supplies stored under their kitchen sink. Part of the Angel Detox involves using only eco-friendly and nontoxic cleaning supplies. You can maintain a sanitary kitchen in ways that are healthful for you and the earth.

Tea tree oil: Pour tea tree oil into a water-filled spray container to use as a general-purpose cleaner and sanitizer. To make it smell better, add geranium oil.

Vinegar: Vinegar is an all-purpose cleaner. Mix water and vinegar to clean floors (test them first for color-fastness) and windows, and for sanitizing.

Eucalyptus oil: Mix with water as a cleaning agent and to clean and prevent mold. You can also use it as an air freshener—either by making a spray or by keeping an oil-heating diffuser in the kitchen.

Baking soda: Use dry, or as a paste mixed with water, anytime you need to scrub while cleaning. Choose organic baking soda that doesn't contain aluminum.

Lavender oil: Wipe on any surface to repel ants and other insects.

Orange peels: Orange is a solvent that cleans grease. To make your own nontoxic cleaner, soak orange peels in salted water for about 30 minutes. Then pour the orange peels and water into a larger glass container and fill the rest of the container with a mixture of half vinegar and half water. Place a lid on the container and allow it to sit unrefrigerated for two to three weeks. Then, strain the liquid and put it into a squirt bottle.

Living a Chemical-Free Life

Almost everything the average person comes into contact with is laden with chemicals. Cosmetics, cleaning products, air fresheners, bug sprays, traffic fumes, water, and food often contain unnatural chemical compounds. The angels ask you to live a chemical-free life as much as possible.

Look for organic products to keep you and your family safe. The pores on your skin are like tiny mouths that drink in the items you use. Choose organic skin lotions, oils, and soaps, as your body absorbs everything you put on it. Make a point of always reading the fine print, and check labels. If you can't pronounce something on the label, chances are it's artificially created.

The angels say it's best to do your research first. If there's a product you're interested in buying, look it up online and check the ingredients list. Call or e-mail the manufacturer to ask if they're using genetically modified products.

★ ★ ★

CHAPTER SIX

"What Should I Eat?"

If you're new to detoxing, you may feel perplexed when you're hungry and wonder, *What can I eat?*

The answer is: focus on the *ingredients* that go into meals more than the meal itself. Many ingredients that you may already have in your kitchen can assist your detox and boost your immune system and energy levels.

It's best to keep meals simple and unprocessed. You don't need to buy those expensive boxed meals that sit for months on store shelves. Those boxes are filled with preservatives and other toxins.

Strive to keep your meals as uncomplicated as possible. Fresh, steamed vegetables; brown rice; and beans make for a satisfying and healthful meal that's easy to digest. Flavor the meal with raw almond butter and your family will think you're a gourmet chef!

Be sure to work the following healthful, detoxing ingredients frequently into your meals:

Garlic

Garlic is a common household ingredient that has incredible healing properties. During my (Robert's) studies to become a naturopath, I had to complete a lengthy assignment on garlic. The essay was long and included over 50 scientific studies to back up its healing effects. By the end of it, I felt that garlic could be used for almost anything! It's so simple, so accessible, yet so wonderfully effective at everything it does.

Garlic helps treat almost every infection you can imagine, starting with the common cold. It's antiviral, to defeat stubborn viral influenzas. It's antibacterial, to balance your digestive health. It also eliminates parasites and other unwanted guests from your body.

Garlic is powerfully antioxidant and protects your cells from damage. It lowers cholesterol by removing unhealthy fats from your arteries and veins. It is antifungal and treats candida along with other yeast-related conditions. It helps lower blood pressure and thins the blood slightly. Garlic even reduces the chemical load on the body by detoxing heavy metals.

Time and again, garlic has been proven to be effective against stubborn bacteria and viruses. Interestingly, research has also shown that the bacteria and viruses have never become resistant to the effects of garlic. In contrast, the bacteria and viruses were able to mutate and protect themselves from conventional pharmaceutical drugs.

Add garlic to your food in order to benefit from its healing and protective qualities. For the best effect, make sure the garlic is as close to raw as possible. Add it to meals at the last minute so it only has a moment to heat before being consumed. You can eat raw garlic on its own, too. First, crush the clove to release the healing compounds, and then soak it in a little water, or put it on a spoonful of food. You need to crush the garlic to combine the alliin and alliinase, which produce allicin—one of the most active compounds in garlic. To alleviate garlic breath, eat a few fresh sprigs of parsley.

I (Doreen) like to make what I call "detox hummus," which consists one can of cooked organic chickpeas (garbanzo beans) combined in a blender with raw garlic, organic olive oil, and seasoning to taste. If you're under the weather, put as much garlic as you can stand into the detox hummus and you'll soon be feeling much better (although your breath may be potent for a couple of days afterward!). I also adore "garlic greens," which are green vegetables such as spinach and broccoli crowns sautéed in olive oil with chopped garlic. So delicious and healthy!

Garlic capsules (containing dried garlic) tend to yield poor results. Try garlic-oil capsules instead for an enhanced effect. You can also use garlic tablets of high quality. Take approximately one to two cloves of garlic a day (four to eight grams). There's also the option of a garlic tincture, but this is not for the fainthearted. The taste is extremely strong and could lead you to lose friends! It brings a whole new perspective to garlic breath. It's still a viable option, but in this case, tablets are a better choice.

The principle of reflexology says that the soles of your feet tell the story of your entire body. By addressing the feet, you can heal the whole system. Following this philosophy, garlic can be crushed and then strapped to the bottoms of your feet. It's great to use for children when they have coughs or colds. Change the cloves every day (or more if you need to), and notice the improvements you see. The garlic gets absorbed through the feet and is sent right up through the body to the place of healing.

Cilantro (Coriander)

Cilantro and coriander are the same herb, but they've acquired different names in different parts of the world. However, they have the same botanical name: *Coriandrum sativum*. You might associate this herb with Thai food. Discover the healing properties of this culinary spice and you'll want to reap its benefits. Due to its essential oil, it helps digestion and upset stomachs. When consumed, cilantro assists in removing heavy metals such as lead, mercury, and aluminum. Your daily activities can expose you to these heavy metals through smoking, paint fumes, chemical-based cosmetics, and air pollution—including geo-engineering weather-modification spraying ("chemtrails").

A small percentage of people find the taste of cilantro repulsive, describing it as soapy and unappetizing. Recent research has found that there's a scientific reason why certain people dislike cilantro so much: it's hardwired into your genetic makeup. So if you don't like the taste of it, consider putting a very small portion in your food from time to time. This will assist with heavy-metal clearing. If you simply can't bear the thought of even a little cilantro, try capsules.

Cilantro and Mercury

Dental amalgams or fillings are a leading cause of mercury exposure, and it's best not to have any in your body. Every time you bite down hard on something, you may be exposing yourself to minute concentrations of mercury vapor. It can be bothersome to have them removed, though, and some dental professionals say that if they're not cracked or leaking, you should leave them alone. However, you might want to speak with a respected dentist if you have any mercury amalgams in your teeth. He or she will tell you if removal is something viable for you. But call on the angels before doing anything. They will guide you to the perfect dentist, and will help you find someone who is empathetic and understands your concerns.

Mercury, like many heavy metals, cannot be removed from your body with normal metabolic functions. Your body needs help to release the buildup of toxic metals. So, even small amounts can build up over time. Mercury has been linked to health conditions such as immune problems, Alzheimer's disease, cardiovascular issues, cancer, allergies, digestive concerns, psychological and endocrine disorders, anxiety, depression, chronic fatigue, learning difficulties, and gingivitis.

Mercury can even protect viruses from medications. It "hides" the virus until the course of treatment is completed. Then, it releases the virus back into the bloodstream. Other heavy metals have been linked to similar scenarios. So, toxic metals can be responsible for recurring infections that seem resistant to treatment.

A doctor happened upon the detoxing abilities of cilantro by "accident," or perhaps by Divine intervention. During some routine tests, he found high levels of mercury. It was higher in the patient's urine after eating a dish prepared with cilantro. This was investigated further, and it was found that cilantro appears to bind to heavy metals. It carries them out of the body and releases them.

Conventional treatments for heavy-metal exposure require harsh chemical methods. They usually cause the patients to feel worse before they feel better. If you feel you may have heavy-metals toxicity, get a test from your doctor or naturopath. If your results show high levels of heavy metals, seek out a holistic physician who works with mineral chelation therapy. Different minerals, such as calcium, bind with heavy metals, like lead. You can receive IV infusions of these safe minerals to quickly and effectively clear your body of toxins. Conventional studies show that chelation therapy has overall health benefits. Your holistic and integrative physician will be able to guide you.

On your own, you can use cilantro to capture the toxic compounds and gently sweep them out of your system. Rather than encountering side effects, you will notice heightened energy, greater clarity, an improved complexion, and a more positive mood.

Consume fresh bunches of cilantro daily, for three or four weeks. This will help your body remove and release any toxic-metal buildup. Add it to smoothies, fresh juices, and as a generous garnish over meals. Prepare salads with a bunch of cilantro leaves as a refreshing lunch or afternoon snack. You can also create a delicious pesto to increase your cilantro consumption.

DETOXIFYING CILANTRO PESTO

2 cups cilantro

½ cup almonds

1 tsp. salt

¼ cup cold-pressed extra-virgin olive oil

Place cilantro, almonds, and salt in a food processor. Combine until the leaves and almonds are finely chopped. Next, turn the processor on and slowly pour in your oil. Done! You can add some cayenne pepper if you like spice. Store in an airtight jar in the refrigerator, and consume within 2 weeks.

Aim to use 2 tablespoons a day. Spread it on sandwiches and toast, or add to freshly cooked pasta. Or, serve as a dressing for vegetables and potatoes. It's important to eat the cilantro in its raw state. If you cook it (like boiling in soups or stir-fries), you denature the important compounds needed for detoxing.

Lemon Juice

The bitterness of lemon makes it an excellent liver-cleansing treatment. Juice half a fresh, organic lemon and add that to a glass of warm water. Drink this first thing in the morning before any other food or drink. As the lemon hits your stomach, it triggers a cleansing process, stimulating digestion and waking up the liver. Your stomach begins to produce acids that will break down your food. Now your body is in the perfect condition to enjoy a healthy breakfast.

Contrary to popular belief, lemons are actually alkaline. They may seem acidic, but once they're digested, they're highly alkalizing. Most illnesses and chronic diseases come from acidic environments. Your body can become too acidic if you consume too much meat and dairy and not enough vegetables and greens. By drinking lemon juice, you're gently nudging your body into an alkaline state.

By juicing two whole lemons (skin and all), you have a very powerful antioxidant medicine. You can add a little locally produced honey or organic coconut syrup to taste if you wish. Take two tablespoons of this mixture each day to fight against the spread of unhealthy cells.

Spirulina: The Green Superfood

Spirulina is an easily digestible superfood. It's a microalgae that absorbs nutrition from the sun and its watery surroundings. When viewed under a microscope, spirulina looks like tiny green spirals. This connects it with the healing emerald light of Archangel Raphael. As you consume spirulina, Raphael is given access to your body and works to dissolve any blockages, as well as increasing your vitality. He opens up your heart with this green energy, as everything that comes from love is healing. Once you get over the initial taste and smell, you'll come to love your green drinks.

Spirulina is one of the most complete nutritional supplements available, containing over 100 nutrients. It's rich in B vitamins, protein, iron, fatty acids, and vitamin A. This is what makes it so beneficial for your body. It requires very little digestion, so even weakened bodies can absorb it.

Spirulina is a strong antioxidant food that helps prevent damage to cells. Antioxidant protection is one of your best defenses against cancer. Scientific studies have shown that the beta-carotene (responsible for antioxidant protection) in fresh fruits and vegetables (including spirulina) is far more effective than that found in synthetic supplements. Your body craves natural sources of vitamins and minerals. Synthetic products may be difficult to break down. Your delicate system can find it challenging to absorb any of the minerals present.

Vitamin B_{12} is necessary for proper brain function and nervous-system actions. Vegetarians and vegans find it difficult to get enough natural B_{12} in their diets. Almost all dietary sources of vitamin B_{12} are animal derived: meat, fish, shellfish, poultry, eggs, milk, and milk products. However, you may choose not to eat animal products due to spiritual or health concerns. Sadly, many B_{12} supplements are made from cow's liver. The products sitting on the health-food-store shelf may contain the animal you're trying to save!

Read the labels carefully to check for bovine or porcine origins. This means that the nutrition is sourced from cow or pig parts. Luckily, nature has given us the superfood spirulina, rich in B_{12}. It's one of the only vegetarian sources of complete B_{12}. In order to receive adequate B_{12} from spirulina, you may have to take more than the bottle specifies. It's always best to consult with a naturopath to choose a dosage that's right for you.

As far as iron is concerned, its presence in spirulina is in an easily absorbed form. It doesn't have the side effects you may be familiar with in other iron supplements.

Spirulina is largely made up of protein, which your body needs for muscle growth and development. Protein is composed of essential amino acids. When digested, protein is broken down by your body to these basic building blocks. Amino acids enhance numerous functions, including energy maintenance, cardiovascular health, concentration, mood balance, pain management, sleep cycle, and nervous-system nourishment. They're also essential for breaking the cycle of addiction. Be sure that you get protein from other food sources, too, such as beans, lentils, and soy. It may be difficult to octain your daily protein needs from spirulina alone.

Spirulina is soothing to your digestive system, as it doesn't require much energy to be absorbed. The food is already broken down to a cellular level and is instantly absorbed. This balances your good gut bacteria. The spirulina serves as a food for probiotic organisms.

Spirulina is wonderful for detoxing, as it removes chemicals, toxins, and heavy metals from your body in a gentle and effective way. Spirulina has also been shown to reduce the harmful effects of radiation. This is further evidence of the protective love of Archangel Raphael.

Spirulina contains gamma-linolenic acid (GLA), which is difficult to find in foods. It's a fatty acid that your body requires for proper nerve function and signaling.

Spirulina also absorbs water in your stomach, which causes you to feel full and satisfied longer. It's great to have in smoothies as a snack, or take it in tablet form prior to eating a big meal.

As you have learned, spirulina has numerous health benefits that include weight management, strengthening the immune system, radiation protection, heavy-metal removal, liver nourishment, and being a source of overall nutrition.

Speak with your naturopath regarding dosage. Generally, a teaspoon of powder mixed with water or juice is taken three times per day. Tablet size/strength will depend on the dosage. Try gradually increasing your amount of spirulina to a spoonful. To begin, try half a teaspoon. Then when you're familiar with the feel and taste, you can increase the amount.

★

A woman named Kristine was diagnosed with fibromyalgia, a chronic condition characterized by pain in multiple locations within the body. Kristine noticed that she was extremely sensitive to a number of foods and environments; in fact, she was having adverse reactions to almost everything she ate. She began to lose a lot of weight and became weak as a result. Finally, she surrendered to God and prayed for help.

The angels and Jesus became her guides and helped her through every step of her healing. She received the message to trust her body; it would indicate what was good for her and what wasn't. The angels began guiding Kristine as to what and how to eat. They would whisper in her ear and tell her which spices to use in cooking, and they'd give her specific amounts to use. Kristine followed and trusted the messages she received.

The angels urged her to intuitively test her food and supplements. What she found shocked her. Most of the supplements she was taking weren't appropriate for her sensitive body. Many of the products were too strong, and her delicate constitution was being overwhelmed. She had a vision in which she saw that she only needed small amounts of vitamins to nourish her cells. This led her to spirulina. Kristine hadn't taken it for a while, but remembered how good it had once made her feel. The easily absorbable nutrition in spirulina made it the perfect guided choice. Kristine began noticing improvements in the way she felt almost immediately. She heard the angels say that soon she would be able to eat a wide range of fresh fruits and vegetables.

Kristine now feels stronger and healthier, as her body can absorb what she eats.

★

Be sure to choose spirulina from reputable manufacturers. My (Doreen's) favorite brands are from Hawaii, where I live. There's evidence that spirulina (and chlorella) made in China contains toxic additives, so it's best to avoid supplements from that country.

Open-Cell Chlorella

Chlorella is another green superfood. It's rich in protein and assists the body with detoxification. Chlorella is one of the most nutrient-dense foods in the world. However, this green algae has a tough outer wall that houses the nutrition. In order for your body to get maximum benefits, the cell wall needs to be broken down. Look for open-cell, or cracked, chlorella supplements.

Chlorella has been studied for its detoxing properties. It was found to be protective against heavy metals such as mercury, lead, cadmium, and copper; as well as PCBs, dioxin, and uranium. After the Chernobyl nuclear disaster, this superfood was chosen to help many who were exposed to radiation poisoning. Chlorella binds with heavy metals like mercury and carries them out of the body.

Chlorella contains something called "chlorella growth factor." This promotes healthy cell growth and supports your immune system. It is also one of the best sources of chlorophyll, the green pigment present in many plants. Chlorophyll enables the transport of oxygen through the body and facilitates the work of hemoglobin. This boosts your energy, restores your red blood cells, and improves your overall well-being.

Superfood Powders

The term *superfood* refers to a food rich in nutrients. It contains many essential vitamins and minerals and will help your body function at its best. In the case of difficult digestion, you want foods that are simple to break down. Powders are useful, as they're readily absorbed by your body. Look for powdered superfoods such as spirulina. There are many products on the market that combine vegetable powders with herbs and superfoods. Visit your local health-food store and see what's available. Our recommendation is to purchase the smallest size first. Test the product on yourself and be sure your body likes it. If you respond well, then you can always buy a larger size in the future. These easily digestible, nutrient-filled foods soothe your gut and raise your vitality.

Green Smoothies for Greater Health

Green smoothies can be a tasty, delicious, and heart-opening experience. They're an excellent vehicle for including more vegetables in your diet. Many people find it challenging to prepare healthy, nutritious meals. Time can often be the excuse that leads people to easy, unhealthy food instead of making something better. Green smoothies are easy, quick, and incredibly nutritious. They can also be an effective way to get good-quality greens into your child's, your teenager's, or even your own diet.

My (Robert's) teenage cousin refuses to eat vegetables (especially green ones!). She will pick them out of her meal, set them to the side, and glare at them as though they've offended her deeply. However, when I make green smoothies, she's the first to line up for a glass. On the one hand, she's repulsed by eating green vegetables, but on the other, she's quite happy to drink them. By doing so, she receives all the health benefits of vegetables in a simple and enjoyable way.

How to Make a Green Smoothie

If you have a high-powered blender, such as a Vitamix, making a green smoothie is very easy. Just pop all your vegetables and fruits in the blender with a little water and ice. Blend on high for a minute or two, and then enjoy. If your blender is unable to break the foods down finely enough, you might need to make it a two-step process.

First, juice any harder foods, such as apples and carrots. Then, add the juice to a blender with soft greens like spinach, kale, or lettuce. If you really enjoy your green smoothies, consider investing in a good-quality, reputable blender. Find one that can liquefy anything it touches, such as the aforementioned Vitamix. Just make sure it's a recent model, which now features BPA-free pitchers. (BPA is a hardening agent in many plastics that leaches out and can create hormone issues, as mentioned previously.) Vitamix and similar blenders powerfully pulverize the food so it's smooth, but keeps all the fiber intact—nothing is wasted.

By blending your greens, you increase the nutritional value. Count how many times you chew your food before you swallow. Chances are it's only a handful of times. The recommendation is to chew your food 20 to 30 times each mouthful. Not many people expend this amount of effort chewing their food, but when the greens are blended, they're already broken down into much smaller particles. This makes it easier for your body to absorb the beneficial nutrients.

Start with smoothies that are a balance of fruits and greens. Then, as your body gets used to the healthy foods you're drinking, you can increase your green content. It's also important to rotate the types of greens in your smoothies. Like everything else in life, moderation is the key. Raw greens contain minute toxins. This is nothing to concern yourself with as long as you vary your greens. So have kale one week—then spinach, chard, dandelion greens, silverbeet, Romaine lettuce, parsley, or rocket (arugula) for a peppery drink. Also, mix up the fruits that you enjoy, but keep it simple, using only one or two a time. It's a great idea to freeze your favorite fruits when in season. We often peel and halve mangoes and bananas and store them in the freezer. This way you can have a ready supply of tasty fruit all year long.

Here's a nice recipe to get started. Be sure to use organic fruits and vegetables:

1½–2 cups kale

½ cup green grapes

¼ cucumber

1 slice of lemon

Flesh of 1 whole mango

2 cups water

Blend all of the ingredients with some ice until smooth. This combination will give you loads of nourishment, detox your body of chemicals and toxins, and also taste good.

The emerald-green color of these smoothies connects to the heart chakra. Drinking green smoothies is a way to love yourself. The energy of the smoothie opens your heart and reminds you to take the time to nurture your soul. The emerald green is also connected to Archangel Raphael, the Angel of Healing. After just a few days of drinking green smoothies, you'll feel lighter, more energetic, and happier. Your heart will sing as you let in the healing energies of natural food.

Enjoy green smoothies as part of your healthy eating plan. You could have one for breakfast, or as a midmorning or evening snack. Then consume healthy, natural foods at your other mealtimes. We're sure you'll enjoy the experience of having green smoothies in your life—you'll learn to love yourself through the magic of greens.

Essential Fatty Acids

The body requires fatty acids to conduct messages along your nerves, but your body is unable to make them, so you must consume them as part of your diet. Some food sources are flaxseeds/linseeds, walnuts, hemp oil, almonds, cold-pressed extra-virgin olive oil, and chia seeds. Include these foods in your diet so that you remain healthy and alert.

Essential fatty acids are natural anti-inflammatories. They nourish and lubricate your joints and provide relief from arthritis by assisting in the fluid movement of your joints.

If you don't get enough of these good fats, it becomes difficult to concentrate. You may feel as if you have a foggy head and are unable to focus. It becomes challenging to remember things as your memory gets worse, too. The brain is made up of fatty tissue; thus, it requires these essential fats to transmit messages. When essential fatty acids nourish your brain, you'll be able to think clearly. A deficiency can also lead to mood swings and increased stress levels. The essential fatty acids help regulate your feel-good hormones.

When you lack good fats in your diet, your body will give you warning signs. Poor-quality hair or problematic skin are examples. Consult with your health-care professional and aim to correct the deficiency by enjoying natural, oil-rich foods. You don't necessarily have to eat fish to get your omegas—which are good fats. Omega-3 is found in linseed, flaxseed, hemp seed, and hemp oil. Omega-6 is found in evening primrose. There are vegan/vegetarian sources of both essential fatty acids.

Oils

To achieve your optimal essential-fatty-acid ratios, you'll want to use oils in your diet. It's important to invest in high-quality oils for flavor and health. The first rule of oils is: never use canola oil! It's an oil derived from the genetically modified rapeseed. There is no "canola" plant in nature. It's a made-up name because marketers know we wouldn't purchase "rape oil." You'll also want to avoid corn oil, since it typically contains pesticides from the genetically modified corn base.

Here are healthful oils to invest in and use in your meals:

Organic extra-virgin olive oil: Numerous studies show the immune-boosting benefits of olive oil. The Mediterranean diet has been associated with a longer life expectancy, and scientists give olive oil much of the credit. Taking olive oil daily has been correlated with the prevention of strokes and type 2 diabetes. There's also scientific evidence that regular olive-oil consumption reduces the risk of osteoporosis and heart disease. Other studies have found that olive oil reduces the risk of skin cancer and also alleviates depression. And the oleic acid in olive oil has been found to prevent breast cancer.

Plus, when you use high-quality olive oil, the taste is delicious! We use olive oil as our salad dressing without any additives. Invest in high-quality, organic, extra-virgin olive oil. Beware of inexpensive brands, which are often counterfeit oils deceptively marked as olive oil. Real olive oil is usually green in color and very thick.

Raw or virgin coconut oil: This delicious oil adds a tropical flavor to your meals, and it can withstand high cooking temperatures. Coconut oil is digestible because its saturated fat is made up of medium-chain fatty acids, which are easier to metabolize and help your body burn fat for energy. The key is to only use non-hydrogenated oils, which are low in saturated fats, such as coconut oil.

In the jar, coconut oil is solid and white, but it rapidly melts into a wonderful texture. You can also use coconut oil as a skin lotion and hair conditioner, and as a treat for pets.

Macadamia nut oil: This delicious and healthful oil has a long shelf life and withstands high cooking temperatures. It makes a delicious salad-dressing oil.

Macadamia nut oil is also rich in antioxidants and protein and can be used a skin and hair moisturizer as well.

Sesame oil: Sesame has been documented as a health agent for at least 5,000 years. In ancient Babylon and Egypt, sesame seeds were used for strength, youth, and beauty. And for good reason!

Several well-documented medical studies have linked sesame oil to reduced risks of cancer, diabetes, and other chronic illnesses. Rich in antioxidants that heal and protect, sesame oil makes a wonderful addition to your meals and personal body-care cabinet.

You can also use sesame oil instead of body lotion to avoid the toxins and high price of store-bought remedies. Just pour in a bit of pure lavender oil to make the sesame oil smell nice as you use it on your body. Sesame oil makes a wonderful conditioner that leaves your hair shiny and smooth.

Raw almond butter: Instead of flavoring your meals with butter or margarine, pour a stripe of raw organic almond butter on food. This butter offers all the health-enhancing benefits of almonds: lowering cholesterol, protecting the heart, and helping prevent colon cancer and Alzheimer's.

Fresh Organic Fruits

If you or your children love sweets, then you'll want to keep plenty of fresh organic fruits on hand. While eating too much fruit can overload your system with fructose (fruit sugar), for the most part you can freely eat it. And fruit is much preferable to other forms of sweets, especially since processed sugar (including beet sugar) is genetically modified.

It's a good idea to keep a bowl of washed organic grapes in the refrigerator for handy snacking.

Fresh Organic Greens

Eat fresh organic greens at least once per day. Healthful greens include kale, chard, spinach, dandelion, arugula, cilantro (coriander), and broccoli. The deeper and richer the green coloring of the vegetable, the more chlorophyll it contains. Chlorophyll reverses DNA damage and protects against carcinogens. Deep green vegetables are a delicious way to protect your health and provide fiber. They're also high in protein and vitamins A and C, and act as anti-inflammatory agents.

Studies show that cooking green vegetables causes them to lose nearly 70 percent of their chlorophyll. That's why cooked vegetables turn gray after a while. So if you do cook your greens, make sure to stir-fry or steam them only lightly so they retain their green color—and their chlorophyll content.

Organic Beans

Organic beans are a healthful source of protein and fiber that can also lend flavor and bulk to your favorite recipes. They're a tasty and inexpensive meat substitute.

Beans don't provide complete amino-acid proteins (with the exception of soybeans), so they must be combined with whole grains such as brown rice for optimal nutritional benefits. If you choose soybeans, be extra careful to only use organic soy products. Genetically engineered or nonorganic soy contains toxins.

You can purchase beans dried and soak them as a way of connecting with our ancestors' cooking methods. Or buy them precooked in cans. We prefer the brand Amy's Kitchen because they have a non-BPA lining inside their cans.

Brown Rice

Many people are gluten sensitive or gluten intolerant, so they need to avoid eating wheat and other gluten products. Signs of gluten intolerance include: exhaustion, bloating, skin issues, irritability, and fertility issues.

Rice is a good grain to substitute for wheat because it's gluten-free. It's important to only choose organic rice to avoid consuming the genetically modified variety.

Brown rice is natural rice. White rice was brown before having its hulls—and nutrients—stripped away.

Brown rice mixed with beans provides a complete protein meal, especially if you eat a side of lightly cooked kale or similar deep-green vegetables. Season the meal with a stripe of raw organic almond butter.

★ ★ ★

CHAPTER SEVEN

7-Day Detox Plans

As we read numerous detox stories, a pattern became clear. When people prayed to God and the angels, they were able to release their addictions. Some people prayed as their absolute last resort, pleading with God for help. Others casually asked the angels for help, and they too received surprising results. No matter what you're detoxing from, prayer always works.

Researchers have long studied the healing effects of prayer, teasing out the variables using scientifically acceptable methods. The most impressive studies show the positive effects of prayer on plants, animals, and infants, who theoretically could not benefit from a "placebo effect" (positive thinking when you consciously know you're being prayed for).

Researchers have shown that prayer is associated with a reduction in reported pain, shorter healing times, increased longevity, and the ability to heal from addictions.

★

By releasing negative influences, a New Jersey man named Jerry Ryan found inner peace. Jerry had long felt his heart calling him to let go of unhealthy habits. He would always start with a plan but never follow through with it. After praying for guidance, he found that he was blaming the world for his issues and wasn't taking responsibility for himself. But then he made the decision to ask more questions and look for greater guidance His faith grew substantially, and Jerry began looking at humanity in a different light. After calling on the angels, he found that there was a great deal to be thankful for. By letting go of the drama and negativity in his life, Jerry learned that anything was possible. Today he gives free music lessons to autistic children.

★

Amanda Dowel noticed clear signs that her energy improved as a result of detoxing. She was guided to start a cleanse where she eliminated all toxic foods. She completed the entire cleanse and felt wonderful afterward: her body felt better, and she had more energy. Shortly thereafter, Amanda had her aura photographed, and the results were all the confirmation she needed. Her aura was bright and clean, with gorgeous orbs in it. By removing toxins from her diet, Amanda gained greater clarity in her energetic field.

★

Shawn McDonald, a Reiki master from California, had a vision of her detox plan. The angels showed her a list of foods and drinks that she needed to release. Shawn laughed loudly, saying to the angels, "Yeah right! Good luck!" On the list were meat and poultry, coffee (which she drank daily), cheese (which she loved), chocolate (which she loved even more than cheese), and alcohol (which she used to numb her feelings).

Shawn wasn't a big meat eater to begin with, so it was the first, and easiest, food to release. She hoped this would give her more time before releasing the next food, although Shawn could sense that a gentle push from the angels wasn't far away.

Making a commitment to clean up her diet led Shawn down other paths. She and her husband chose to stop resisting the changes that the Universe was guiding them to make. They surrendered to the moment and let God take charge. At the time, they were struggling to keep their home in the Bay Area. Shawn was also keeping her spirituality a secret. They were guided to move to the town of Capitola with their young daughter. They'd both been very drawn to this place and often visualized themselves living there. The transition was smooth and positive for all of them.

Immediately, Shawn embraced her spiritual gifts and started sharing them with others. She soon opened her own healing practice, where she guides clients on their journey.

Gradually, over the course of a year, all the foods on her list disappeared from her diet. Shawn now enjoys ginger, lemon, and water as a replacement to her morning coffee. She makes treats for her family, but uses carob instead of chocolate now. She also makes them gluten-, soy-, and sugar-free, too!

Shawn prayed for help in releasing alcohol. In the past, she was using it as her crutch to escape the guidance from her angels, but she realized that she was ready to fulfill her life's purpose. The process of detoxing from alcohol came slowly. First, she could only tolerate cutting back to a couple of glasses of wine. After drinking she would feel heavy, and more open to psychic attack. The angels stepped in to answer her prayers. After a couple of months, the craving for alcohol vanished! Shawn woke up one morning and the idea of alcohol was almost unbearable. She no longer had any desire for wine whatsoever.

She now realizes that these foods weren't removed from her, they were removed *for* her! Shawn prayed for help from her angels, and they answered the call. She is now much happier—having made the transition to being caffeine-, gluten-, and soy-free, and adopting a vegan lifestyle. In the beginning, Shawn thought this would be impossible, but she now realizes that making these changes was essential for her so that she could fulfill her destiny.

★

Rebecca Rogers, a busy mother of three, is a nurse at The Canberra Hospital in Australia. Rebecca wanted more energy, so she continually told herself that she needed to have the greatest amount possible. Unbeknownst to her, the angels were listening to her prayer.

Rebecca went to the supermarket as normal, but this time was attracted to the vegetarian section. She'd become so bored with the foods she was cooking, so she thought it might be fun to try something different. She purchased soy milk, soy yogurt, loads of fresh fruit and vegetables, healthy grains, and no meat. Overnight Rebecca stopped eating dairy, meat, fish, and eggs.

Initially, she experienced symptoms of her body cleansing itself. She had headaches but refused to take pain pills. Rebecca knew that her body was detoxing from chemicals and didn't want to introduce more. She received wonderful help and guidance from compassionate friends on the Internet, who all urged her to keep going, as the benefits would be amazing.

Even though this has been a very recent change, Rebecca is feeling better physically, mentally, and spiritually. She received the answer to her prayers for high energy!

★

Nancy A. Kerner had received help from the angels in the past. Twenty-three years ago, she asked God to release her craving for drugs and alcohol—and He did! But now, at this point in her life, she wanted to detox from certain foods.

Nancy was unhappy living in Seattle, as her body desired more sunshine. She wanted to move to California, but she knew the move would involve a lot of work and planning, as her family would have to pack up their home and retail business. So, Nancy prayed for help, asking for a miracle. She said she was ready and willing to do what it took to heal her body, and asked for guidance to bring her body back into balance and health.

Within five weeks, she received the money her family needed to get a condo and retail space in California—all within walking distance of her 80-year-old father.

Nancy enjoyed the warmth and sandy beaches as she watched dolphins and whales play in the ocean. This heightened energy allowed her to easily release sugar, coffee, and fast food. During meditation, she received the guidance to go vegan and gluten-free. Nancy had no plans to do so but thought she would try it out. She enjoyed green smoothies, coconut water, and fresh juices. Even her husband was enjoying the vegan meals she prepared.

Now, each day Nancy lights a candle and prays. She asks for guidance and support as she continues making positive life changes. She is so grateful for her newfound health. She's lost weight and can even run up the stairs now.

★

Tracy Moldovan, a pharmacist, prayed for help for her son, Nickolas, who was a sick little boy. He'd been having different neurological tics that occurred over a three-year period. It started with rapid eye movements and developed into sniffing, head jerks, and loud throat clearing. He would do this every 10 to 15 seconds for many hours throughout the day.

Tracy knew that the common treatment for this condition was antipsychotics. But as a pharmacist, she knew about the horrendous side effects these drugs could have and vowed that she'd never give them to her child. She also prayed for help and was guided to a physician trained in environmental medicine. This led to a hair mineral analysis. The results were staggering, showing that Nickolas was in complete muscle breakdown. He was found to have high levels of aluminum in his body, which affected his nervous system. Tracy chose to switch to organic food to avoid further toxin exposure.

Through continued prayer, Tracy was guided through each step of Nickolas's healing. Friends and co-workers would suggest books or documentaries at the perfect time. They gave Nickolas a fish-oil supplement as well as vitamins. And Tracy eliminated candy, artificial colors, and preservatives from the family's diet.

The year before, Nickolas would have been diagnosed with Tourette's syndrome. There's currently no known cure, and the prognosis is very sad. Today, Nickolas doesn't have any tics. He is healthy, growing, and turning into an amazing boy! His future potential is unlimited.

★

Lisa Watterson lived on processed junk food. She consumed loads of salt, sugar, caffeine, and processed foods. Not surprisingly, her body was unwell. She often had symptoms of irritable bowel syndrome (IBS), headaches, bloating, pain, and tiredness, to name a few.

Lisa was always connected to her angels. However, it wasn't until Christmas when she received my (Doreen's) book *The Angel Therapy Handbook* that she learned to ask for help with detoxing. Lisa was astounded. Why hadn't she thought of calling on the angels to help her with her diet? When she did so, she instantly could feel her body shift. She found that when she ate unhealthy foods, they gave her no satisfaction. She started to crave fruits and vegetables, and she was guided to begin regular exercise.

Lisa now has more energy and feels fantastic!

Soda and Soft Drink Detox

So many people are addicted to soda and soft drinks, which are loaded with artificial flavors, sweeteners, and sugar. These items are certainly not going to improve your health or your clairvoyance. In fact, the ingredients in cola leach minerals from your body. So not only does cola not add anything to your health, it also reduces health-enhancing calcium and magnesium! Clearly, soda is not your friend!

High consumption of soda can lead to frightening conditions such as high blood pressure and cholesterol, obesity, and insulin resistance. Some researchers suggest that drinking large amounts of soda puts your body under the same stress as alcohol. If abused for long enough, this may lead to liver damage, which becomes a concern as more and more children become addicted to these sweet, sugary beverages. Children aren't the only ones drinking these products, but the angels are worried about the future health of the next generation.

Diet soda is just as harmful. From a naturopathic point of view, artificial sweeteners in diet soft drinks cause a multitude of issues. They also make your body believe it's having a sugar rush. However, when your body tries to counteract the high level of sugar, nothing happens. Hence, your body becomes stressed and struggles to understand what's going on. It continues to produce more substances to lower your blood sugar; however, the brain retains the message that the sugar levels are too high. This carries on for hours until the artificial sweetener leaves your body.

Many people choose diet soda as a means of weight loss, but there's research to suggest that weight loss is delayed by artificial sweeteners. So the very thing you thought was helping you may be hindering your process.

The artificial sweetener in diet soda is called aspartame, which is also sold under the brand names Equal or NutraSweet. This chemical should be illegal because it's toxic. It breaks down into highly toxic methanol, which further breaks down into formic acid and formaldehyde. These chemicals affect nerves, and have been shown to lead to migraine headaches, nervousness, and even seizures. Studies on rats have shown that aspartame is linked to congenital birth disorders.

In addition, sodas are bottled in aluminum cans, and that dangerous metal can leach into the beverage. When soda comes in a plastic bottle, it most likely contains BPA, a hormone-disrupting chemical found in most plastics.

These drinks prevent you from hearing the guidance of your angels and damage your clairaudient (psychic hearing) abilities. Overall, soda makes all communications with the higher realms fuzzy.

The angels have shown us that soda damages your aura. It looks like tiny bubbles of acid that dissolve your auric shield. When you drink soda, your aura becomes weakened and more prone to psychic attack. Your aura is a gift from God, as it helps you stay shielded and protected from lower energies. It's your first line of defense against negativity. However, if this layer of protection is weakened, it becomes easier for negative energy to enter, which can cause fatigue, anger, irritation, and mood swings. You can also observe this in children when they're labeled as ADD or

ADHD. If they're taken off soda, they can deflect the lower energies in their environment, and soon these soda-free children start to concentrate better.

We asked if it's all carbonated beverages that do this to the body and aura. The angels said no. They explained that good-quality carbonated mineral water is okay (although some brands contain too much sodium, which can lead to bloating).

Sodas are acidic to the body, which means they have an acidlike effect. The angels confirm that the drinks eat away at your protective shield, and the acids in soda can leach needed calcium from your bones. This makes the bones more brittle and leads to an osteoporosis-type condition.

It's alarming to see so many children drinking large quantities of soda. The angels warn that they may end up with poor bone strength as they age. It's also well known that the acids in soda can break down tooth enamel. It's said to be more damaging to teeth than sugary foods alone. The acid helps the sugar penetrate the teeth more deeply.

Juice: The Healing Drink

Enjoy natural drinks as alternatives to soda. You may find that it takes a week or two to really enjoy natural beverages again. Your poor taste buds have been damaged by long-term exposure to this harsh chemical substance. Over time, your mouth will thank you by bringing back a heightened sense of taste. Choose fresh juices made from organic fruits and vegetables, which you can enjoy in a number of ways. Having your own juicer is a great way to go, as it allows you to customize your juice to suit your personal taste preferences. There are several kinds of juicers available: the centrifugal, auger, and blender.

The centrifugal juicer is the most common variety. It contains a fast-moving part that has a grating action. It quickly shaves off the fruit and vegetable and allows the juice to fall through. These kinds of juicers produce a large amount of "waste" (which is beneficial fiber, laden with nutrition), and a small amount of juice. This is often the least expensive form of juicer.

The auger-type juicer, also known as a masticating juicer, contains one or more slow-moving parts that crush the fruit or vegetable. These juicers produce a lot more juice and allow you to enjoy items like wheatgrass and other green leafy vegetables. Cleaning is often easier, as there is less waste.

The third form of juicing is our favorite—the blender. Blenders allow you to enjoy fresh fruit and vegetable juices with the whole food. This means that nothing is wasted, and you benefit from the full complement of fiber and nutrition that the food contains. Do some research on juicing blenders. You'll find that the more you spend, the better quality you'll receive. I (Doreen) have used a Vitamix blender for years as a way of making beverages and meals from the whole plant, instead of throwing away the fiber as traditional juicers do.

With a blender, you can mix organic fruits like mango, grapefruit, and apple with carrots, spinach, and broccoli. Add some ice and a little water and you have a fresh, healthy drink. Your body will be far more appreciative of this kind of beverage. In comparison, soda has a harsh, abrasive energy.

Some organic juices to try:

- Kale
- Beet
- Pineapple
- Mango
- Grapefruit
- Watermelon
- Carrot
- Apple
- Spinach
- Almonds (nonirradiated)
- Banana

In addition to consuming juice, you can add a slice of lemon or lime to your water. This makes it more interesting and enjoyable to drink. And you can add a tiny amount of fresh fruit juice to add flavor.

Healing Methods to Detox from Soda

Prayer

"Dear God and angels, please support me on my journey toward greater health. I am now ready to release soda from my diet. I can understand your messages and wish to follow your guidance. I hope to hear, see, feel, and know your Divine presence around me. I know that this can only happen if I detox from this unhealthy, processed food. I pray that you help me release soda, and any cravings associated with it. May my health improve immediately and my energy be repaired. Thank you."

Archangel Michael's Spiritual Vacuuming

Soda weakens the aura and allows negative energies to come in. These low vibrations often continue your cycle of addiction. Work with Michael to clear your body of negativity. (See Chapter 1.) At the same time, you'll be releasing your need for soda.

7-Day Plan to Detox from Soda

For each of the detoxes in this chapter, we provide you with a seven-day plan. The angels say to use this as your starting point. Allow your intuition to guide you, and make appropriate adjustments based on your situation. At the end of the seven days, you're asked to continue following your own individual detox path. Call on the angels and ask questions of knowledgeable sources for further guidance and support.

Day 1

- Begin your day by thoughtfully saying the "detoxing from soda" prayer. Continue to repeat this prayer throughout your day, especially at mealtimes. When you visit places where you frequently drank soda in the past, call on the angels for help. The key to your success is remembering to ask for their Divine guidance.

- Enjoy a healthy bowl of organic oats such as muesli or porridge. These complex carbohydrates will help you feel satisfied longer, without the urge to grab a soda for a pick-me-up.

- Dispose of any soda you have in your home. By eliminating temptation, you'll have greater success. Waste food isn't ideal, but gifting harmful "foods" to others is really no gift at all.

- Purchase natural, organic juices as well as ripe fruits.

- Say the "detoxing from soda" prayer before bed.

Day 2

- Begin your day by thoughtfully saying the "detoxing from soda" prayer. Snack on organic raw almonds if you have any cravings for soda.

- Flavor your water with organic juices and citrus fruits.

- Monitor your feelings and emotions today. Your ego may try to trick you into drinking soda. Call upon your angels for strength and support to release it from your life.

- Meditate with Archangel Michael, and perform his spiritual vacuuming technique. Continue this practice daily for the rest of the week. Also ask Michael to vacuum your refrigerator and the areas where you drank soda. This lifts the old energy and enhances your motivation.

- Say the "detoxing from soda" prayer before bed.

Day 3

- Begin your day by thoughtfully saying the "detoxing from soda" prayer.

- Start drinking the herbal tea calendula today. It will repair your aura and strengthen your psychic shield. The soda has degraded your auric field, so this an excellent time to begin healing it.

- Be more aware of your protein intake today. Enjoy beans, lentils, and soy protein sources. This increased protein will stabilize your blood sugar. Consider having a protein shake made from soy or pea protein to curb low energy levels.

- Say the "detoxing from soda" prayer before bed.

Day 4

- Begin your day by thoughtfully saying the "detoxing from soda" prayer.

- Give yourself a treat for making it this far. The hardest part is already over, and everything from this point on will be much easier. Create your own fizzy beverage by combining puréed fresh fruit and berries with sparkling mineral water.

- Say the "detoxing from soda" prayer before bed.

Day 5

- Begin your day by thoughtfully saying the "detoxing from soda" prayer.

- Make time today to vacuum again with Archangel Michael. You're already becoming more sensitive to energy and hearing the guidance of your angels. By vacuuming, you keep these psychic channels clear.

- Enjoy freshly squeezed juices today. Blend healthy organic greens like spinach with fresh apple, carrot, and ginger juice.

- Say the "detoxing from soda" prayer before bed.

Day 6

- Begin your day by thoughtfully saying the "detoxing from soda" prayer.

- Keep yourself busy today by cooking. Choose a meal to prepare that takes some time to make. Give each step your time and love. By doing so, you'll appreciate the end result. Your taste buds are beginning to heal and give you a greater sense of taste. As you eat today, be mindful of the flavors and textures of foods. They will be vastly different from last week.

- Say the "detoxing from soda" prayer before bed.

Day 7

- Begin your day by thoughtfully saying the "detoxing from soda" prayer.

- Spend time with loving, supportive friends. If you happen to go out for lunch, enjoy herbal teas or water as your drink of choice. It's important to stay diligent in your decision to release soda from your life. The angels are supporting you, and have been supporting you all week.

- Work with Archangel Michael's spiritual vacuuming technique to release the energy from the day.

- Say the "detoxing from soda" prayer before bed.

Congratulations! You've gone an entire week without soda! Already your taste is improving, your aura is strengthening, you've saved money by not buying soda, and you can begin to hear the messages of your angels again.

Alcohol Detox

Look at hand sanitizers and hospital-grade disinfectants. What is the main ingredient? Alcohol or ethanol. This is because alcohol is a poison! It's excellent for killing bacteria and germs, as they can't live when exposed to it, and the very same process is occurring at the human cellular level. Your body is made up of millions of cells, each of which is sensitive and necessary. If your body didn't need them, it wouldn't have made them. (The one exception here is cancer cells.) Alcohol can damage and kill your essential cells, and another frightening fact about it is that it's able to cross the blood-brain barrier. Most drugs and chemicals are ushered through the body to the liver. There, they're metabolized and processed so they don't cause you greater harm. Alcohol skips this and heads straight for the brain, where your delicate nerves are exposed and fragile.

Alcohol weakens the aura and allows negative energies to come in, making it easier for unwelcome spirits to attach themselves to your body. If you black out from alcohol, these spirits create health concerns and pain. Alcohol is a poison, and your energy field responds to it as such. It will look thinner and less stable than it once was.

When people die, they might carry their addictions with them. If you frequent bars and clubs, these places are filled with the souls of deceased alcoholics. Through your weakened aura, they attach to you and live out their cravings through you. Therefore, you'll notice an increase in your desire to drink and will want to make it part of everything you do socially. Other telltale signs are being clumsy, dropping things, and bumping into walls. If you think you have a spirit attachment, do a vacuuming with Archangel Michael. He will escort the lower beings to the light.

Our prayer is to shine light on addictions and help you heal them. The more "sober" we all become, the brighter the world looks. We aren't here to make you feel bad. Our goal is to point out what may happen, and give you ways to overcome your addictions.

If you do drink, surround yourself with loving individuals. Your weakened aura loses strength as negativity from others attaches itself to you. You may feel emotions such as anger, fear, anxiety, depression, or hate. Clearly, clubs, pubs, and bars are not good places. They're filled with lower energies and earthbound spirits who are trying to continue their addictive behaviors.

Many people associate alcohol with being social. After all, you don't want to be the only person not drinking when everyone else is having a good time. But when your energy is high, you don't need alcohol to enjoy yourself. You can replace alcohol with your own "mocktails" to join in. For my (Robert's) 18th birthday party, I drank nonalcoholic mocktails. My friends and guests saw me having a great time and assumed I was drunk. I'm not sure if it's a good or bad thing to admit that I was 100 percent sober and just as entertaining.

Enjoy drinking sparkling mineral water mixed with fresh organic juice. Try pink grapefruit, watermelon, or kiwi. Squash some fresh raspberries, blackberries, blueberries, or strawberries in a glass and top with sparkling mineral water. Or blend ice with tasty fruits like mango and peach for smoothies. Enjoy healthy, natural beverages that keep your aura intact and your energy high.

If you feel that alcohol is something you struggle to control, please get the help and support you need. Your angels may have been urging you to seek help already, and this is your confirmation. Look for your local Alcoholics Anonymous meeting or visit www.aa.org to find a 12-step program near you.

★

A woman named Sue Ogozarek woke up on January 2, 2007, shaking from alcohol withdrawals. She was in an unfamiliar house with a man she didn't know. She had four children, but there was a Protection from Abuse (PFA) order against her, and Sue was currently homeless.

She was sick and tired of her life. She thought about committing suicide but worried about what that would do to her kids. Her mother had committed suicide when Sue was six years old, and she remembered that pain all too well.

She got on her knees and prayed for help from God—she was willing to receive it in any way, shape, or form. All she had with her was a duffle bag with two pairs of sweatpants in it because her husband had become so irritated by her drinking and other behavior that he'd thrown her clothes away.

Sue had to leave this man's house, but she had nowhere else to go. It was raining and cold outside, so she went to a bar. Sue had sworn that she wouldn't ever go in this particular bar, as it was full of older men, but she nevertheless went inside and sat next to someone. He looked vaguely familiar, like someone she knew from a previous bar. She had no money and asked this man to buy her a drink, which he did.

The stranger asked her about her duffle bag. Sue explained it was all she had and that she was homeless. The man asked why she didn't call her parents. Sue told him that her mother had died when she was six, and she hadn't spoken to her dad in over ten years. Sue and the stranger chatted for several hours; then miraculously, and in answer to her prayers, Sue's dad entered the bar at that exact moment! They reconciled, and he asked Sue to live with him, promising to take care of her. He checked her into rehab, and Sue hasn't had a drink since.

The stranger Sue sat next to was a good friend of her father's. Upon hearing her story, he called her dad, who lived an hour away. That man had never been to this particular bar until that day, but for some reason he was guided to go there and help Sue. Now Sue knows that in addition to her dad, God, her mom, and the angels are looking out for her. She is enjoying a sober life that now includes her children.

★

A woman we'll call "A.H." prayed for help in detoxing from alcohol. At the time, she was a waitress at a bar. One evening she had a little too much to drink and came home dizzy. Her stomach was twisted and sore, and she felt like she was going to vomit. A.H. endured this discomfort for three hours before breaking down in tears, realizing that there was nobody to help her.

She called on God and prayed to have all alcohol removed from her body. Within seconds, she felt a strong energy enter through the top of her head and travel down to her stomach. A.H. felt that this energy was gathering up all the toxins from her body. Suddenly, she felt the energy rush toward her mouth as she physically released the alcohol. Feeling so relieved, she chose sobriety as her only option.

Over the course of that evening, A.H. detoxed from alcohol and never looked at it again. She called on God in her time of need, and He delivered His healing prescription.

★

Brenda Pennington slipped into alcoholism after a painful divorce at the age of 44. Prior to that time, she'd never touched alcohol. Now she was using it to mask the pain and trauma she was feeling. She wanted help, and the angels delivered.

Brenda moved to California, where she met an Angel Therapy Practitioner. She began attending this woman's monthly angel gatherings and learned how to heal her emotions. This was a sensitive time, but she knew she had to face her feelings in order to truly heal. During this process, Brenda realized she needed to detox from alcohol. She prayed for help and asked the angels to take away her cravings.

In the initial stages of her detox, Brenda was guided to sleep outside under the summer stars so she could bathe in their healing light. This touched her soul very deeply and gave her the strength to let go of alcohol and other old addictions. It was a miracle! Not only that, but she was given a $7,000 scholarship to learn about healing modalities of her choice! Today, Brenda enjoys vibrant health as she shares her healing journey with others.

Healing Methods to Detox from Alcohol

Prayer

"Dear God and angels, please help me now. I need your guidance and support. Please assist me in detoxing from alcohol. I want to release it, and all of its negative effects, from my life completely. I can see the impact it has made on my life and the lives of my loved ones. Please, I pray that you take away all my cravings for alcohol, and all temptations in my path. Through this process, I will learn to love myself. From a place of unconditional self-love, I know I will heal from this. Thank you."

Essential Oils

Lavender oil calms the mind, clears the third eye, relaxes the nervous system, and uplifts the spirit. Allow this oil to permeate your home by diffusing it in an aromatherapy burner. You can also place a single drop of lavender on your pillow to aid sleeping.

Lavender gives your brain time to override the need for alcohol. If you've told yourself that alcohol calms you, then use lavender to calm you instead. Its purifying energy detoxes negative influences, and it clears your environment so that low-energy people fall away from your circle of friends.

Rose essential oil inspires self-love. Rub a single drop over your heart area and feel the energy penetrate your soul. When you love yourself, you won't do anything to yourself that causes harm. Your Higher Self knows that alcohol is preventing you from greatness, as it leaves you feeling unmotivated and sluggish. The rose energy gives you a comforting hug that lets you know that everything will be okay. It heals judgments you've passed over yourself and focuses on positive outcomes.

Archangel Raphael's Addiction Release

Call upon Archangel Raphael to release your need for alcohol. Many people have reported that they've instantly given up alcohol after saying this prayer. (See Chapter 1.) Be honest and authentic with Raphael, and allow him to help you.

Milk Thistle, or St. Mary's Thistle
(*Silybum marianum*)

Milk thistle heals and protects the liver, and gives it nourishment to repair the damage caused from alcohol. Don't use the alcoholic tinctures and extracts of this herb. Instead, work with glycetracts, tablets, or capsules. Glycetracts are non-alcohol-based extracts of an herb that are preserved with glycerin and taste sweet. They're a good alternative for alcohol-dependent people, as they're alcohol-free, which gives you flexibility with respect to the dosage if you're guided to have more or less milk thistle. Tablets and capsules are another great option that are easy and convenient. Most tablets contain concentrated extracts of the herb, which is more than you'd be able to tolerate as a liquid. Follow your angels' guidance, as well as the advice offered by your health-care professional.

Vitamin B$_{12}$

Frequent users of alcohol almost always have low B$_{12}$ levels because alcohol decreases this vitamin's absorption. Consider taking a B$_{12}$ supplement to rebalance this important vitamin. Most B$_{12}$ supplements are taken sublingually, meaning under the tongue. They often come as a dissolvable tablet or liquid spray. Studies have shown that B$_{12}$ can be better absorbed under the tongue compared with injections.

B$_{12}$ is needed to focus your thought processes. If you lack this vitamin, it's hard to form happy, loving thoughts. When you fall into a dark space, alcohol is an easy temptation, so lift your spirits and your energy by taking B$_{12}$. But if you do so, please take it in conjunction with a balanced B complex/multivitamin. If individual B vitamins are taken in isolation, they can cause deficiencies.

Zinc

Over 400 reactions in the body are dependent on zinc. It has a strong connection to the nervous system, as well as the skin, immune system, reproductive system, and digestive system. Zinc is needed to perform various metabolic reactions. If you're deficient in zinc, these reactions can't take place.

When detoxing from alcohol, zinc intercepts the addiction cycle. It heals your nervous system, regulates the messages coming from your brain, reduces cravings, and balances your mood.

7-Day Plan to Detox from Alcohol

Day 1

- Start the day by saying the "detoxing from alcohol" prayer with heartfelt intention. At any point during the day when you feel you need extra guidance and support, repeat the prayer.

- Dispose of all alcohol. You can throw it in the trash; however, it's a powerful release to pour it down the drain. As you watch it disappear, feel its previous hold on you being released.

- Call on Archangel Raphael to work with his addiction-release process. Sever the attachment to alcohol now and forevermore.

- Ask for help from compassionate people. It's important to have a supportive network around you as you're detoxing. You may feel guided to attend an AA meeting or confide in true friends. This is essential as you progress on the road to recovery. Remember, it's okay to ask for help and call a friend when in need.

- Before bed, repeat the "detoxing from alcohol" prayer.

Day 2

- Start the day by saying the "detoxing from alcohol" prayer with heartfelt intention.

- Vacuum with Archangel Michael to release any lower energies or entities attracted by the alcohol. Also ask him to vacuum any places where you used to drink. Place a bunch of white roses in your home to purify the area of unwanted spirits and negativity.

- Let the scent of lavender essential oil permeate your home to bring about peace and tranquility. It's perfect in the evenings to promote relaxation and restful sleep. Many people drink alcohol to wind down from the day. Let lavender be of service to you in this regard by taking away your cares and concerns.
- Before bed, repeat the "detoxing from alcohol" prayer.

Day 3

- Start the day by saying the "detoxing from alcohol" prayer with heartfelt intention.
- Consider starting a zinc supplement. Provided you have no other health concerns or medications you're on, aim for 50 to 60 mg of zinc per day. Take it at a different time from your other supplements, as it can interact with them and prevent them from being fully absorbed. Ideally, take the zinc at night just after dinner.
- Carry a hematite crystal with you to affirm your cleansing from alcohol. Anytime you feel low, hold the hematite in your hands and feel the support and love around you. Remind yourself that it's okay to ask for help. Include your angels in every step of your detox.
- Before bed, repeat the "detoxing from alcohol" prayer.

Day 4

- Start the day by saying the "detoxing from alcohol" prayer with heartfelt intention.

- Place a drop or two of rose essential oil in your palms. Rub them together and then lovingly place them over your chest. Inhale the aroma and feel your heart open. Know that you deserve love and that you can release any past pain, guilt, or negativity.

- Bring iris flowers into your home. They will detox you and clear away the energy of addiction. If you can't find fresh irises, you can print some photographs of them from the Internet, as images of the flowers have the same potent energy.

- Before bed, repeat the "detoxing from alcohol" prayer.

Day 5

- Start the day by saying the "detoxing from alcohol" prayer with heartfelt intention.

- Start taking B_{12} today. Provided that you're not on other medications or have other health concerns, go with a dosage of 1,000 mcg of B_{12}. You must balance your other B vitamins, so always take a B complex/multivitamin as well as your B_{12}. This ensures that your B's stay in proportion to each other. The B_{12} will help you think more positive thoughts as you release alcohol.

- Before bed, repeat the "detoxing from alcohol" prayer.

Day 6

- Start the day by saying the "detoxing from alcohol" prayer with heartfelt intention.

- Develop and maintain a regular exercise plan. It's essential that you let your body sweat, which will allow you to release old toxins that build up in your body. Perhaps include a friend in your exercise regimen for additional support.

- Before bed, repeat the "detoxing from alcohol" prayer.

Day 7

- Start the day by saying the "detoxing from alcohol" prayer with heartfelt intention.
- Now it's time to begin your liver healing. Take milk thistle every day for at least three months. Take a tablet or liquid glycetract. Follow the directions given for the tablets, or take 25 drops of the glycetract three times a day in a little water. This herb gently cleanses your liver and helps it function at its best. If you're on other medications or have other health concerns, speak with your health-care provider before starting milk thistle.
- Before bed, repeat the "detoxing from alcohol" prayer.

You've already gone an entire week without needing alcohol. Take this time to reflect on the improvements that you're already experiencing as part of this detox, and carry them with you as you move forward with an alcohol-free life.

Wheat and Gluten Detox

Wheat is an overly used grain that can be found in almost every processed food. It's what we make flour from. Flour is often added as a thickener and dispersing agent in packaged food. For example, wheat is in potato chips since it's used in the seasoning. It's found in animal products like sausages to bind the meat to-gether. This increases the size of the end product, too. It's all too commonly overconsumed.

When we eat too much of any food, or eat it too often, the-body creates inflammation. We do best when on a rotational diet, as explained in Chapter 2. This means that we eat something, then avoid that same food for a number of days; that way, we digest and properly absorb the nutrients. Your body will thank you for avoiding the same foods and reward you with heightened energy and increased vitality.

The most reactive substance in wheat is gluten. The angels liken gluten to "glue." They say that it causes your cells to stick together, which makes your body work harder than it should. It sticks to the inside of your third eye, like gum, which prevents you from receiving clairvoyant insights.

Gluten is also found in barley and rye. Many people who are intolerant of gluten are also intolerant of oats. Oats do have gluten; however, it's different from that found in wheat, rye, and barley. Oats are often contaminated with additional gluten by being processed in facilities that also process these other grains. Being aware of your sensitivity to oats and gluten is something that can only be discerned through trial and error. Please follow your body's responses and the guidance you receive from your angels. You may be able to enjoy eating porridge and muesli, or you may have to avoid all foods containing gluten.

Many people don't realize that they're intolerant of gluten. Your angels may have been urging you to stay away from breads, cakes, and pasta, but you might have thought this was to avoid excess carbohydrates or to lose weight. More likely, though, you've been receiving this guidance because your precious body has difficulty processing gluten.

Blood tests can be performed by your doctor or naturopath to identify this intolerance, but these tests can sometimes be expensive. If you feel you're sensitive to gluten, avoid it—remove it from your diet completely for a month. Then, check in with your Higher Self and notice the difference. You'll be able to hear your angels more clearly, and you'll find that your energy levels have increased. Your cravings for excess carbohydrates will disappear, and if you had stomach or digestive issues, these will likely be resolved, too.

To make it crystal clear, you can test yourself. After avoiding gluten and wheat for four weeks, eat them again for one week. Notice the changes you experience in your body and also in your mind. Many people will experience digestive disturbances, bloating, and a foggy head; concentration becomes harder as the gluten clogs your brain functions. Your connection to the angels will start to cloud, and you'll definitely know to steer clear of gluten.

A lesser-known compound in wheat is gliadin, which many people are sensitive to as well. Gliadin is a glycoprotein found in wheat and other grains containing gluten, and it has been linked to several immune responses. A review conducted in 2012 by the National Cancer Institute in Italy found that gliadin caused negative immune responses, and did so once it hit the intestines. Australian wheat is high in gliadin, making it sought after by bakers, as it provides the desired light, fluffy texture when used. This, however, is more likely to cause an immune reaction within the body.

So eat grains that are low in gliadin, and vary the grains you eat. If you must eat wheat, choose those products that are imported from Italy. Semolina, the flour used to make pasta, is a hard form of wheat that's low in gliadin. This is less likely to cause your body discomfort. A safe alternative is rice pasta, as there's no wheat or gluten in rice, and the taste is almost the same.

Enjoy other alternatives to wheat such as:

- Almond meal
- Cornmeal (must be organic to avoid GMO)
- Coconut flour
- Rice flour (must be organic to avoid GMO)
- Besan, or gram, flour (from chickpeas)
- Flaxseed meal (must be organic to avoid GMO)

Wheat can also be hidden in condiments such as soy sauce. A tasty wheat-free version is tamari. It tastes almost identical, without the negative immune reactions.

★

A woman named Jessica Ann Parke discovered the power of detoxing in 2002. She learned about removing unhealthy foods and substances from her diet. Yet it wasn't until 2007 that she realized she was gluten intolerant.

Jessica always felt peaceful and serene when detoxing. Then, as she reintroduced foods, she noticed significant changes in mood. The most severe reactions related to gluten and wheat. If Jessica ate any gluten products at all, she'd feel drastic psychological effects, such as anxiety, depression, confusion, and anger. All of those symptoms vanished when she detoxed from gluten. But if she accidentally ate any gluten, she would instantly have mood swings and become emotional.

Now that she's removed gluten completely from her diet, Jessica is thinner and healthier. Her face looks clearer and less puffy. Best of all, she no longer looks tired.

As a result of releasing gluten, Jessica has seen a marked increase in her intuition. She noticed improvements with her psychic abilities and became more empathic. She can better focus and concentrate now as well. Her gluten-free diet has made her more peaceful overall so she can hear the voices of her angels.

Healing Methods to Detox from Wheat and Gluten

The angels are very happy to help you release wheat, gluten, and gliadin from your diet. Trust your Higher Self and inner guidance. Is releasing these substances for your highest good? If so, this is part of your Angel Detox.

Prayer

"Dear God and angels, please lift out the glue from my aura. I understand that wheat and gluten are impacting my abilities. I choose this moment to willingly release all forms of wheat. I choose to release gluten now. Please heal my body and my energy. Thank you for this healing."

Archangel Raphael Meditation

Find a quiet space to sit. Begin by centering yourself through calm breathingt. As you take slow, deep breaths, set the intention to listen to your body. Be willing to hear what your sensitive temple has to share. When you feel ready, ask your body, "Will I benefit from removing wheat and gluten from my diet?"

Sit quietly and wait for an answer, which may come as a thought, feeling, vision, or voice. Trust this answer. Next, ask your body, "What benefits will I experience from releasing wheat and gluten?"

Listen for the response. Take this moment to ask any other questions regarding your relationship with wheat and gluten. Now call upon the benevolent and healing Archangel Raphael by saying:

"Dear Archangel Raphael, please help me remove wheat and gluten from my diet. Please guide me to release these foods without cravings or withdrawals. Please remind me to ask if foods contain gluten, and to check package labels for wheat. Archangel Raphael, surround my body with your healing emerald light to dissolve any attachments to this substance now."

Visualize images of wheat, flour, breads, cakes, and other gluten-containing foods being erased by the loving light of Raphael. When the healing is complete, thank Raphael for his support. He will stay with you as you detox from these substances, and will protect you from the unhealthy effects of gluten from now on.

Goldenseal (*Hydrastis canadensis*)

Goldenseal repairs the lining of your stomach. Over time it strengthens your digestive system and heals "'leaky gut" syndrome. This occurs when you continually eat the foods that you're intolerant of. As you do so, the lining of your stomach becomes weaker and thinner. This poor-quality membrane allows toxins to be reabsorbed into your body. Goldenseal repairs this damage and reduces inflammation.

You may be able to introduce small amounts of the intolerant food back into your diet, but it will take several months before your body will be ready. You must eliminate the food entirely and work with goldenseal. Then, you can test by trying small portions. Trust the messages form your body, because you may be guided to avoid gluten for life.

Probiotics

Good gut bacteria are essential for proper digestion. As you detox from wheat and gluten, you need to repair your digestive system. The gluten can slow your bowel, which makes it easier to hold on to toxins. When you have a digestive system that's balanced with healthy bacteria, you can easily eliminate waste.

Take probiotics just before you eat, and look for those varieties that need to be kept in the fridge, as they will give you the best results. Also check to see which good bacteria these products include. Aim for a product that contains a broad spectrum of probiotics, not just one or two. If you do the research, you'll find probiotics that contain about eight different strains per dose.

7-Day Plan to Detox from Wheat and Gluten

Day 1

- Start the day by saying the "detoxing from wheat and gluten" prayer. Continue saying this prayer during the day as you feel you need extra support from the angels.

- Remove all wheat-containing products from your kitchen. Without wheat in your home, you won't accidentally ingest it. Tune in to other gluten-containing foods and ask your Higher Self if you need to dispose of those, too. For some, all gluten will need to be removed immediately. For others, you'll begin with wheat and then may feel guided to release all forms of gluten in the future. Trust your feelings, and listen to the messages you receive.

- Find a quiet space today to speak openly with Archangel Raphael. Conduct his meditation exercise described previously to gain further insight into what wheat and gluten do to your body. You may want to write down the information you receive so you can refer to it over the next week.

- Shop for wheat alternatives at your local health-food store. You can find nutritious grains and pulses that are wheat- and gluten-free.

- Say the "detoxing from wheat and gluten" prayer before bed.

Day 2

- Start the day by saying the "detoxing from wheat and gluten" prayer.

- Gluten binds your cells together like glue. Ensure that you hydrate well today by drinking plenty of water. This flushes out old toxins and built-up proteins from your system.

- Research gluten-free recipes and relevant cookbooks. Going without gluten doesn't mean that your diet has to become boring. You can still enjoy healthy, delicious meals every day! Ask your gluten-free friends to share recipes or suggest menu choices.

- Say the "detoxing from wheat and gluten" prayer before bed.

Day 3

- Start the day by saying the "detoxing from wheat and gluten" prayer.

- Over time, your high intake of wheat has damaged your digestive system. Start repairing your gut by taking a probiotic supplement. Probiotics contain good bacteria that balance your digestive health.

- Good fats are important for energy and brain function. Keep up your great work by adding avocados, coconut oil, and walnuts to your diet.

- Say the "detoxing from wheat and gluten" prayer before bed.

Day 4

- Start the day by saying the "detoxing from wheat and gluten" prayer.

- Today is an excellent day to reacquaint yourself with your spiritual gifts. Take time to meditate in solitude to identify your true self. Even 15 minutes can make a big difference in your day and on your outlook on the future. By spending more time meditating, you will connect with the Universal energies that are available to heal you.

- Work with Archangel Michael to clear your energy and home with his spiritual vacuuming technique. This makes the energy around you much more peaceful and balanced. In your new sensitive state, you deserve a clean environment and body!

- Give your digestion a kick start by drinking fresh lemon juice. First thing in the morning (before you eat or drink anything else), squeeze half a lemon into a glass of warm water. Drink this to stimulate digestion and prepare your stomach for the arrival of food. The bitterness of the lemon heals digestive upsets as you release gluten.

- Say the "detoxing from wheat and gluten" prayer before bed.

Day 5

- Start the day by saying the "detoxing from wheat and gluten" prayer.

- Goldenseal heals and repairs the lining of your digestive system. Start taking ten drops of goldenseal tincture three times per day. Add this to a small glass of water or juice, and drink just before food. If you have other health concerns or are taking additional medications, please speak with your health-care provider first.

- Enjoy fiber-rich foods that cleanse your digestive system, such as green leafy salads and fresh fruits. Your bowel has been sluggish and lazy due to the wheat. Now it's time to remind it of its role in your health.

- Say the "detoxing from wheat and gluten" prayer before bed.

Day 6

- Start the day by saying the "detoxing from wheat and gluten" prayer.

- Check in with your energy levels and feelings today, and notice the difference. Already you're seeing the world through clearer eyes. This planet is a wonderful place to be! See love wherever you travel, and bless all whom you encounter.

- Dandelion tea enhances your liver function and digestion. Start drinking this herbal tea today to ensure that all toxins are leaving your body. You can add a little honey or agave nectar to sweeten the tea if you desire.

- Say the "detoxing from wheat and gluten" prayer before bed.

Day 7

- Start the day by saying the "detoxing from wheat and gluten" prayer.

- Today, prepare a hearty meal of lentils. These protein-rich pulses will give you nourishment and contentment. They're abundant in fiber, which will clean out your digestive system, satisfy your brain, and lift your spirits.

- Say the "detoxing from wheat and gluten" prayer before bed.

Tune in to your health and acknowledge the benefits you're already noticing. Continue looking brightly toward the future, and embrace the new and exciting health improvements to come!

Dairy Detox

Dairy clogs up your third eye and creates a film over your chakras. By consuming dairy products on a regular basis, you reduce your ability to clearly hear your inner voice. As you know, milk is used to create cream, butter, and cheese. Cheese is a concentrated form of milk that can quickly block your psychic abilities. If you've been struggling to connect with your angels, check your cheese intake. When you release cheese from your diet, your intuition is instantly heightened.

As humans, we're the only species who drinks another animal's milk. Your body is designed to process human milk—not that of cows, goats, or sheep. As such, you may experience symptoms from your dairy intake, including stomach pains and bloating. The most common complaint, though, is the production of mucus. This makes you constantly clear your throat, suffer from sinus pain and headaches, and look ill. Small children (and adults) with constant runny noses do very well when they detox from dairy.

These days, especially in the U.S. and Canada, dairy products are genetically modified unless they're certified organic. The dairy cows in North America are fed genetically modified grains, and the toxic pesticide residue is then transferred into the milk products. In addition, most factory-farmed cows are injected with antibiotics and growth hormones, which enter the milk supply.

Also, the cruelty involved in breeding factory-farmed dairy cows gives the resulting dairy products the low-energy frequency of pain and suffering, and you ingest this energy when you drink or eat dairy products from mistreated cows.

One of the cruelest facts about dairy farms is that cows must be lactating to produce milk. That means that calves are immediately taken away from their mothers, because the milk is being sold, instead of given to the baby animals, as nature intended. Imagine if your baby was whisked away moments after its birth—what cruelty to both mother and child!

But it gets worse: the male baby cows won't produce milk, so they're put into tiny, cramped cages called "veal crates." These cages ensure that the baby won't produce muscle, so that it can be killed and sold as "veal," which is another name for young male cows who were treated inhumanely. The energy inherent in eating veal is about as low as it gets.

Skin issues such as eczema are linked with dairy intake, too, and acne is much worse in those who ingest a lot of dairy products.

Milk must be pasteurized by law. This process kills any bacteria or parasites that could be present. However, many feel that it's the homogenization process that causes problems—this makes the milk uniform so it no longer separates into cream. Doing so damages the protein in milk and creates inflammation in the body. You can try unhomogenized milk, although you may find it better to detox from it completely. This "old-fashioned" milk is similar to that which your grandmother received on her doorstep and doesn't cause the severe reactions conventional milk does.

Good-quality yogurt doesn't trigger intolerant reactions like other forms of dairy products do. Perhaps this is because of the good bacteria that digest lactose. If you're guided to release dairy, you can wean yourself, or your child, by eating natural, organic yogurt. Do so for a few weeks as you introduce dairy replacements.

There are many alternatives to dairy, such as soy products, but make sure that the soy you eat isn't genetically modified. You can enjoy organic soy milk, cheese, yogurt, and even ice cream. Almond, hemp, oat, rice, and sunflower milk are also delicious alternatives to dairy. In fact, the new vegan cheese brands made from almond milk actually melt when cooked! Carob is a dairy-free alternative to chocolate, but again, be conscious of food labeling, as some brands include dairy solids such as casein.

How to Make Your Own Almond Milk

Making your own nut milk is so easy! All you need is raw organic almonds (or other preferred nuts), water, and a blender. Put a cup of almonds in a bowl and cover with water. Leave them overnight to soak. In the morning, discard the water and place the almonds in a blender. Add in three cups of chilled springwater. You can also include a date for sweetness. Or, add a pinch of cinnamon and a splash of vanilla. Turn the blender on high, and process until everything is smooth and combined. Strain the almond milk by pouring it through some cheesecloth, muslin, or other strainer. It keeps in the fridge for three or four days.

If you don't have time or forgot to soak the almonds overnight, you can make a fast nut-milk blend: Mix organic raw nuts in a high-speed blender with filtered water. Add organic vanilla powder if desired. The chunky nut milk is perfect poured over cereal or granola. Or, you can filter the mixture using cheesecloth (health-food and online stores sell materials to filter the nuts from the milk).

You can use the same method for cashew or sunflower milk.

Hummus Instead of Cheese

I (Doreen) detoxed myself from cheese by substituting hummus for it. I haven't had cheese since 1996, and I don't miss it at all! I also credit releasing cheese for my crystal clear clairvoyance.

Hummus is a spread made from tahini (sesame paste), garbanzo beans (also known as chickpeas), olive oil, and sea salt. You can easily make hummus in your high-powered blender, or buy premade organic varieties. Add in your favorite extras such as garlic, red peppers, olives, cilantro, marinated artichoke hearts, or sundried tomatoes. You can use hummus as you would cheese.

Some stores now sell delicious organic vegan cheese substitutes that actually melt and brown. Look for them in your health-food store's deli or dairy case. But make sure that it doesn't contain casein, a milk protein that often leads to allergic reactions in lactose-intolerant people. The presence of casein means that the product is not truly vegan.

Calcium Intake

There's no need for any concerns about calcium. When you detox from dairy products, friends and family members may pester you with questions about your calcium intake. Only people who eat animal products need to supplement with calcium, because animal products leach this mineral from your body. You can get adequate calcium from other food sources such as kale greens. If you're guided to do so, you can supplement with calcium to ensure that your body is getting the nutrition it needs.

Sesame seeds have high levels of calcium. Add them to salads and stir-fries. How do you eat enough sesame seeds to get a good amount of calcium? Tahini. If you haven't used tahini before, it's like peanut butter, only made with sesame seeds, not peanuts. Tahini spread on gluten-free toast drizzled with agave nectar is a tasty, nutritious treat. Use tahini in salad dressings to incorporate more calcium in your diet. Or use it as the basis for a delicious and nutritious hummus spread.

Dark-green leafy vegetables are rich in calcium, too. Spinach, kale, watercress, mustard greens, and seaweed are calcium-friendly foods. Broccoli is another calcium-rich green to enjoy.

Healing Methods to Detox from Dairy

Prayer

"Dear God and angels, please dissolve the film of dairy covering my aura. I pray for greater clarity and a stronger connection to you. Please detox my body from dairy, and all its effects.

I am willing to release dairy now, and I ask for your help. Guide me to let it go without cravings or difficulty. Please show me healthy foods that are rich in calcium so I can properly nourish my beautiful body. Thank you."

Archangel Metatron's Sacred Beam of Light

By calling on Metatron, your chakras will be balanced and realigned. (See Chapter 1.) This strengthens your connection to the Creator. Clear away the film and mucus that dairy has left on your energetic body.

Archangel Raphael's Addiction Release

Raphael would love to help you release dairy in all its forms. Raphael, in his benevolent wisdom, will hold your hand as you proceed.

Archangel Raphael Meditation

Sit quietly and take slow, deep breaths. Take this opportunity to listen to your body. Be willing to hear what your magnificent body has to say. When you feel ready, ask it, "Will I benefit from removing dairy from my diet?"

Peacefully wait for an answer. The message may come as a thought, feeling, vision, or voice. Trust your answer. Next, ask your body, "What benefits will I experience by releasing dairy?"

Listen to your body. The body is your best divination tool, as it knows all. Ask any other questions regarding your relationship with dairy. Now call upon majestic Archangel Raphael by saying:

"Archangel Raphael, please help me let go of dairy. Please guide me to release it without cravings or withdrawals. Please remind me to ask if foods contain dairy, and to check package labels for milk products. Archangel Raphael, surround my body with your healing emerald light to dissolve any attachments to this food now."

Visualize images of milk, cheese, cream, and other dairy-containing foods being released by the loving light of Raphael. When the healing is complete, thank Raphael. He will stay with you as you continue to detox, and protect you from the unhealthy effects of dairy from now on.

7-Day Plan to Detox from Dairy

Day 1

- Say the "detoxing from dairy" prayer first thing in the morning. This will help you as you go about your day, so be sure to repeat it as often as needed.

- Clear out all dairy products from your home. Remember to look at any packaged items that may have dairy solids or cheese powder in their ingredients.

- Sit in peaceful meditation with Archangel Raphael. Use the preceding meditation exercise to gain further insight into how dairy is affecting you. Learn, directly from the angels, how you can overcome these products and their ill effects.

- Before retiring for the evening, soak one cup of raw almonds in a bowl of water, and let them sit overnight.

- Repeat the "detoxing from dairy" prayer before you go to sleep.

Day 2

- Say the "detoxing from dairy" prayer first thing in the morning.

- Start your day by making some almond milk! Take your presoaked almonds from last night and rinse them thoroughly. Add the almonds to a blender along with three cups of water. You can add a spoonful of honey or agave nectar for sweetness. Or, leave your almond milk unsweetened. Blend the ingredients on high for two to three minutes. When complete, strain the pulp by pouring the milk through a piece of muslin cloth or a stainless-steel strainer. (You can use the pulp for baking, or you can leave the pulp in to retain fiber.) Store in the fridge and consume within a few days. This is a tasty and nutritious alternative to cow's milk.

- Work with Archangel Raphael and perform his addiction-release exercise. Raphael happily assists you in letting go of your addiction to dairy products and eliminating temptations and cravings.

- Repeat the "detoxing from dairy" prayer before you go to sleep.

Day 3

- Say the "detoxing from dairy" prayer first thing in the morning.

- Monitor your diet closely and ensure that you include calcium-rich foods. Make salad dressings and dips from tahini. Steam broccoli for lunch and dinner. If you're worried about your calcium intake, you can consider a supplement. However, first sit in meditation and ask your angels if this is truly right for you.

- Repeat the "detoxing from dairy" prayer before you go to sleep.

Day 4

- Say the "detoxing from dairy" prayer first thing in the morning.

- Overeating dairy products has clogged your aura and blocked your chakras. Release this film by calling upon Archangel Metatron and working with his sacred beam of light.

- Eat and enjoy hummus spread.

- Repeat the "detoxing from dairy" prayer before you go to sleep.

Day 5

- Say the "detoxing from dairy" prayer first thing in the morning.

- Spirulina is nutrient dense, heart opening, and healing. Begin by taking one teaspoon today. Mix it with a glass of organic, freshly squeezed juice; and slowly increase your intake as you feel guided. Progress to taking one teaspoon two or three times daily, then increase the spoon size.

- Repeat the "detoxing from dairy" prayer before you go to sleep.

Day 6

- Say the "detoxing from dairy" prayer first thing in the morning.

- Consider taking a quality multivitamin. If you've been eating a lot of dairy, your body is accustomed to receiving calcium, vitamin D, vitamin A, and vitamin E. As you detox from dairy, your body will naturally pull you to healthy foods that are rich in these nutrients. It's still a good idea to supplement with a multivitamin to make sure you're getting enough.

- Repeat the "detoxing from dairy" prayer before you go to sleep.

Day 7

- Say the "detoxing from dairy" prayer first thing in the morning.

- Gather some red or pink roses and bring them into your home. Photographs are just as effective if you're unable to find fresh blooms. Sit in front of the flowers and send healing energy to all the cows and other animals that are inhumanely treated. Pray that others follow your example, and choose ethical manners of obtaining calcium to support their body. Feel the flowers open your heart and take away any pain you may have ingested. Release the toxins and lower energy from dairy products into the light.

- Repeat the "detoxing from dairy" prayer before you go to sleep.

Dairy has been released from your life, and your spiritual gifts are reawakening. Enjoy your natural psychic abilities, which are much clearer now. You've removed the film that was blocking your spiritual sight.

Sugar Detox

The angels have shown us that sugar crystallizes in the aura. It forms tiny white granules on the lining of the energetic shield. These sugar crystals deplete you of energy and drain you of motivation and vitality. They prevent you from completing important tasks and lead to procrastination. The angels have also said that they're responsible for headaches, as they pull energy out through your head, and sensitive lightworkers can feel this. These headaches can only be healed through the removal of sugar from your diet. Taking pain pills won't help in this case, as they trigger headaches that worsen with sunlight. The more sugar you consume, the bigger these crystals become. Conversely, as you detox from sugar, the sugar crystals shrink and vanish.

Archangel Raphael can help speed the process along. Work with him by saying:

> *"Archangel Raphael, please wash away the sugar crystals in my aura."*

Visualize Raphael spraying warm water over your aura. Sugar dissolves in warm water. When you cannot see any more in your aura, thank Raphael for the cleansing.

Sugar comes in many forms. Natural sugars, found in fresh fruits, are balanced with fiber. Fiber slows the absorption of sugar into the bloodstream. This delay prevents "sugar spikes" from occurring. Instead, you get longer, sustained energy.

When you ingest refined white sugar, you get a lot of calories all at once, and your body rushes to find balance. You release chemicals and hormones to regulate your sugar levels, and this rush of energy is quickly followed by a sugar crash. Your blood sugar drops as fast as it spiked, and your body pays the price. You can become tired, moody, and irritable.

If you don't burn off the calories you consume, you store them as fat cells. So, if you ingest high levels of sugar for long periods of time, you'll gain weight. Eating refined sugar also triggers an addiction cycle that makes you crave more. This cycle never leaves you feeling satisfied, but only serves to perpetuate itself.

Here's a scenario to help you understand this cycle. It explains the role of sugar intake and blood-sugar levels in the cycle of addiction:

You start the day by eating a bowl of sugary cereal. It fills you up for a little while, but soon afterward, you're hungry again. Your body has quickly absorbed the sugar, giving you energy. Then, just as quickly, it drops to nothing. This triggers your brain to think it needs more energy. You hear that as a call for sugar. So, hunger kicks in and you search for a snack. You find some cookies and chocolate to "satisfy" you. Again, soon afterward, you're hungry. By now your brain chemistry is being affected, and your moods start to deteriorate. And it's not even lunchtime yet! What you put in your body is directly correlated with your energy levels. By choosing to eat natural, unprocessed food, you will beam with vitality.

Natural sugars that are found in fresh, whole foods are nourishing to your body. They give you energy and can help reduce cravings for processed sugar. So enjoy eating fresh, high-energy fruits—tropical summer varieties are particularly delicious and sweet. Plus, they're much healthier than candy bars.

People get worried about the consumption of fruit such as bananas, because they're higher in sugar than other foods. But remember that there's also fiber in the banana. Your body processes this kind of sugar differently. Unless you're diabetic, you can enjoy a wide range of tasty fruit, as it's an excellent snack to satisfy your sweet cravings.

If you're guided to stop eating chocolate, you're probably a highly sensitive person. The chocolate industry is filled with pain energy, as it's the main one utilizing slave labor. If you do eat chocolate, only buy brands that are labeled "Fair Trade," meaning that everyone involved in the manufacturing process was fairly treated and paid.

I (Doreen) was guided to stop eating chocolate in 1995 because I was getting headaches. While I was praying for guidance, the angels showed me that chocolate was lowering my vibrations. I asked for help and immediately lost all my cravings for chocolate. I haven't eaten any since 1995, and I've never had another headache!

★

A woman named Megan Elfertasse was aware of her unhealthy addiction to sugar for years. She had a strong desire to detox from sugar but didn't know what to do about it.

Megan's angels showed her the harmful effects of sugar and warned her that she could become diabetic. Her inner voice told her that sugar was pure poison for her body. In the past, she'd been oblivious to the ways in which it affected her. Now, Megan began to see that sugar depressed her, and enveloped her in a mental fog. It also caused mood swings that were affecting the way she behaved as a mother. It brought her extra aches and pains, making her body feel worse. Megan was most frightened when she realized that sugar was weakening her intuitive abilities so she couldn't hear the messages of her angels.

The angels urged her to join Overeaters Anonymous (OA) to release sugar from her diet. Megan continually prayed to Archangels Michael and Raphael for help. They gave her the courage to join OA. Instantly, she heard the message that she needed to change her life. Sugar was giving Megan the same biological response that alcohol gives an alcoholic. Now she was ready to make a change.

At first she held the belief that she'd never be able to release sugar, so she opened her heart and prayed to the angels. She asked them to take away her cravings for sugar so she could regain her sanity, health, and life. It worked! The angels released Megan from her sugar addiction. She started feeling a sense of calm and peace even when the option of sugar was available. She felt inflammation leaving her body, and her mind became clear.

Archangel Michael continues to support Megan, giving her constant reminders of what sugar can do. She is now able to maintain her serenity and make positive, loving choices.

★

Jane Powell, a former drug-and-alcohol counselor, saw the effect sugar had on her body. To begin with, she didn't know how to detox. People kept encouraging her to eat sugar at parties and gatherings, and she listened to her ego when it said she deserved a sweet treat such as cupcakes. But her Higher Self knew that sugar was creating chaos in her body and mental state.

One day Jane realized that she needed to treat her sugar addiction like any other. Just as she'd counsel others going through a drug-and-alcohol detox, she needed to follow the very same principles. Jane remembered that a psychic had told her that Archangel Michael was with her. Her husband, a police officer, assumed Michael was there for him, as Archangel Michael is the patron saint of police officers and all those who work in service to others. Jane called on Michael and asked him to release her addiction to sugar. She felt an urgency to detox from it right away. She removed all sources of sugar from her home and cleared it out of her life. With the loving support of her husband, Jane overcame her addiction and detoxed her life.

★

Kirsti Boothroyd, an Angel Intuitive from Brisbane, Australia, realized her body was a sensitive tool, and that it would clearly show her its reactions to certain foods.

After eating a small packet of cookies, Kirsti noticed the effect it had on her. Instantly she felt tired and cranky. But out of boredom, she kept eating the same foods. She didn't realize the effect that processed, high-sugar foods could have. Each day Kirsti felt lethargic and miserable due to the sugar she ate. Then, she noticed that her daughter's behavior was linked to her sugar intake as well. She would throw tantrums and be difficult to console. At the time, Kirsti didn't know that it was the additives in the sugary snacks that triggered this behavior.

The angels gave Kirsti the guidance to quit her high-sugar diet and provided her with the right tools to do so. Overnight, she stopped eating all sugar products. Intuitively, she knew that sugar didn't agree with her sensitive body. Now that they no longer eat sugary food, both Kirsti and her daughter enjoy peaceful, harmonious energy.

Healing Methods to Detox from Sugar

Prayer

"Dearest God and angels, I'm ready to release sugar. I know that now is the perfect time for me to detox from this substance. I trust in your guidance and your love. I know that you'll help me through this and lead me away from temptation. I ask for your Heavenly presence to surround me. Sugar is so readily available, so I need your support. Keep me strong and healthy. I don't want to feel the negative effects that sugar produces, so I willingly choose to release it now. Thank you."

Sweet Rewards

Children are often given sweets as rewards for good behavior, so they soon associate sugar with pleasure. Studies show that infants always choose sweetened water over the plain variety.

Scientists believe this is an instinctual response that gives us the ability to select ripe fruit in the wild.

If you frequently crave sugar, you might be really craving rewards! Perhaps you feel that you're always doing the giving and not receiving acknowledgment or gratitude.

Sugar cravings can also be a sign that you need to have more fun. When was the last time you played? By introducing fun hobbies into your schedule, you may find that you don't desire as much sugar. This is a simple and natural way to feel better, lose weight, make new friends (if you join a fun club or class), and even start a new business!

You can also help your children avoid sugar addictions by rewarding them with praise, fun trips, toys, or other noncaloric treats.

Natural Sweeteners

You may be able to use natural sweeteners in moderation. Energetically they don't pose the same threat as white sugar. However, overconsumption can lead to weight gain. Try organic forms of agave syrup, honey, raw coconut syrup, or stevia. They make wonderful alternatives to sugar. And, they provide sweetness. If your insulin levels are prone to fluctuation, choose raw coconut syrup or crystals.

Before using any form of sweetener, consult with the angels to see if it's right for you. Sit quietly and ask:

"Is it okay for me to use natural sweeteners such as agave, honey, or stevia?"

Listen for the answer. Your body will receive the message as visions, thoughts, words, or feelings. You owe it to yourself to trust the guidance you get. If you feel that you should avoid these options, trust the messages you receive.

Archangel Michael's Spiritual Vacuuming

Work with Archangel Michael to clear your body. Vacuuming will release lower energies and balance your moods. Unbalanced moods can be caused by sugar energy. Let Michael take this away for you and bring you happiness. He knows that the process of detox needn't be trying or painful, so let him release cravings and discomfort. He will bring Divine balance to your body and energy.

Archangel Raphael's Addiction Release

Raphael wants to help you release processed sugar, which he views as an unnatural, manufactured substance. It's unlike the natural sugars found in fresh produce. Let Raphael take away the need for sugar and help you release food and drinks high in this substance.

Archangel Raphael Aura Wash

As explained earlier in the chapter, ask Raphael to cleanse your aura of sugar crystals.

Chromium

Chromium regulates blood sugar and prevents sugar cravings. It increases your body's sensitivity to sugar so that you can no longer tolerate it. If you do eat sugar, it will taste overpoweringly sweet to you. It's an excellent way to wean you off sugary foods.

To achieve optimal results, the dosage needs to be high. There are also different forms of chromium: some are better absorbed, some are only for short-term use, and others can't be taken in high amounts. It's safest to consult with your naturopath to get the right product and dosage for you. Always check with a professional before starting something new.

Gymnema (*Gymnema sylvestre*)

Gymnema has incredible sugar-regulating properties. It balances blood sugar and removes cravings. This herb numbs the sweet taste buds and decreases the body's absorption of sugar. It's an exquisite action that no other herb can perform. So, if you take gymnema and then eat sugary foods, you'll receive no satisfaction—the taste changes and you won't like it.

Here's a fun experiment: Place a few drops of gymnema tincture on your tongue. Swallow it and then put a quarter teaspoon of sugar in your mouth. At first you might not notice it, but the sugar will have absolutely no taste—it will feel like sand in your mouth!

Gymnema has been studied for its beneficial interaction with the pancreas. As mentioned, it regulates blood-sugar levels. But gymnema also works on specific cells in the pancreas to make this happen. It's a remarkable herb that deserves respect.

Magnesium

This nutrient will help you when you exercise a lot, because when you do so, your body uses carbohydrates for fast energy. If you do intense exercise regularly, you burn through your carbohydrate stores. Your body wants more energy, so it gives you cravings, and the foods that often look appealing are high-calorie, sugary items.

By taking magnesium, these cravings can be removed. It nourishes your muscles, giving them fuel from a nonsugar source.

7-Day Plan to Detox from Sugar

Day 1

- Spend a few minutes repeating the "detoxing from sugar" prayer in the morning. Repeat this during the day to feel the constant support of your loving angels.

- Sit in solitude with Archangel Raphael and conduct an addiction release. Feel the old energies that were tying you to sugar being dissolved by Raphael's healing presence.

- Enjoy complex carbohydrates today. Start your day with a healthy bowl of oats—porridge or muesli. These complex grains will give you sustained energy over several hours. If you start the day with a sugar-filled cereal, or a sweet treat during your coffee break, you'll fight fatigue all day long. Your blood sugar will go up and down, and you'll crave even more sugar. By enjoying complex carbohydrates, your body and energy will thank you. Continue this practice throughout the week and during each day.

- Use your intention as you repeat the "detoxing from sugar" prayer before bed.

Day 2

- Spend a few minutes repeating the "detoxing from sugar" prayer in the morning.

- Take time for personal reflection today. During this time of tranquility, ask your Higher Self if you're able to have natural sweeteners such as stevia, agave, or honey. Trust the initial response you get, and follow this guidance.

- The indulgence in sugar has crystallized in your auric field. Wash away these harmful energies by working with Archangel Raphael. Notice how your sense of energy and vitality instantly improves!

- Use your intention as you repeat the "detoxing from sugar" prayer before bed.

Day 3

- Spend a few minutes repeating the "detoxing from sugar" prayer in the morning.

- Clear away any negative energies you've picked up. Archangel Michael's spiritual vacuuming technique will detox you from spiritual debris that was attracted to the sugar.

- Carry snacks with you to satisfy your hunger. Always keep a small jar of nuts and seeds nearby to nibble on through the day. This will prevent you from munching on something unhealthful.

- Use your intention as you repeat the "detoxing from sugar" prayer before bed.

Day 4

- Spend a few minutes repeating the "detoxing from sugar" prayer in the morning.

- Chromium reduces cravings for sugar and balances your blood sugar. To achieve this result, aim for 600 to 800 mcg of chromium per day. Take it in equal doses spread throughout the day—that is, at least 200 mcg at breakfast, lunch, and dinner. Check with your local naturopath or health-food store to ensure that the type of chromium you wish to take is safe. Some forms are more easily absorbed and can be harmful if the amount is too high. Remember to practice safety first. Also be sure that your health-care providers are aware of any desire you have to introduce other supplements into your diet.

- Satisfy your sweet tooth by enjoying natural, organic, freshly squeezed juices. You can purchase a juicer and create fabulous blends of your own—this process is rewarding and delicious! Freshly squeezed juice is best enjoyed immediately; however, you can add a little juice to your water bottle and sip it through the day.

- Use your intention as you repeat the "detoxing from sugar" prayer before bed.

Day 5

- Spend a few minutes repeating the "detoxing from sugar" prayer in the morning

- Gymnema is an excellent herb to quell sugar cravings and regulate blood-sugar levels. Start taking 12 drops of gymnema tincture three times a day. Add the drops to a small glass of water and drink before eating food. If you encounter challenges with sugar cravings, you can increase your dose to 20 drops, three times a day. Please be mindful if you're already taking medications or have other health concerns. You must always check with your health-care professional before starting something new.

- Monitor your protein intake, and make sure you're getting enough. Protein helps slow the absorption of sugars and therefore releases cravings. So, examine your diet and be sure you're consuming enough protein to satisfy you.

- Use your intention as you repeat the "detoxing from sugar" prayer before bed.

Day 6

- Spend a few minutes repeating the "detoxing from sugar" prayer in the morning.

- Magnesium regulates your nervous system and also has a sugar-regulating effect. If you crave carbohydrates after exercise, then start taking a magnesium supplement. Think about taking 400 mg of elemental magnesium each day, 200 mg in the morning and the remaining 200 mg in the evening. As always, check with your health-care practitioner first.

- Use your intention as you repeat the "detoxing from sugar" prayer before bed.

Day 7

- Spend a few minutes repeating the "detoxing from sugar" prayer in the morning.

- Create and maintain an enjoyable exercise routine. Your body needs to sweat to release stored toxins, but it also needs physical movement. By exercising, you achieve the high energy and happiness you thought you were getting from sugar. Sugar cannot make you feel better, although the ego will do its best to convince you that it will. However, only God and the angels have the ability to bring you joy. As you exercise, you release stress and become more in tune with the high vibration of Source energy.

- Use your intention as you repeat the "detoxing from sugar" prayer before bed.

You're already enjoying the sweetness of life by detoxing from sugar. Your body and your angels thank you! You will receive higher energy and greater clarity as your aura is cleansed and balanced.

Caffeine and Coffee Detox

Caffeine is a stimulant that can be found in coffee, tea, soda, and guarana. When you consume it, your nervous system becomes excited and gives you a false perception of energy. The energy from caffeine isn't pure—it makes your body work harder physically and mentally. Your body is the best tool you have to identify your needs. When you're tired, it's asking for rest. You may need more sleep, or need to find another form of relaxation. Caffeine picks you up and makes you get back to work faster. It depletes your energy levels and can make you feel even more tired as a result.

Energetically, caffeine creates spikes in your aura. Rather than looking smooth and secure, your aura becomes jagged and sharp. It's harder for you to sense the energy of people and places. You only get little "taste tests" of energy. Unknowingly you're putting yourself at risk.

Caffeine makes your chakras, which filter energy, spin faster. They absorb energy and simultaneously send energy out. Like an air-conditioner filter, the chakras become blocked and need clearing from time to time. You can work with Archangel Michael's vacuuming technique very effectively, but caffeine makes the chakras work overtime. They don't get a chance to process the energy before they send it out again. You can feel confused and irritable as a result.

★

Suzanne Slaw was addicted to coffee. She'd started drinking it when she was a teenager, and later in life, it caused her to be admitted to the emergency room.

At the age of 17, Suzanne left her hometown and started attending a new school. The timetable was drastically different from what she was used to. The first class started at 7:35 A.M., so she turned to coffee to wake her up in the morning. Her reliance on caffeine continued throughout college—it was the elixir that got her through her midnight cramming sessions.

Suzanne's coffee addiction became more evident when she started working as an elementary-school teacher. She couldn't begin to comprehend anything going on throughout the day unless she had a cup of coffee in her hand. Suzanne even put a mini coffeemaker in her classroom so coffee would be readily available. Now she could brew herself a strong cup to get through the afternoon.

Eight years later, she was working in the hospitality industry. She sat at a desk for ten hours at a time, only getting up to get another cup of coffee from the café. She thought it was her fuel and her only source of energy. (In truth, God is our Source, and only He can awaken us.)

One morning at work, Suzanne felt flushed. She became weak and short of breath, and her heart began to race uncontrollably. She informed her supervisor, who immediately called 911. Rescue personnel quickly arrived and took her blood pressure and heart rate. Suzanne had a heart rate of 226 beats per minute—the average is 60 to 70 beats per minute. Her heart was beating more than three times every single second! The ambulance rushed her to the nearest hospital emergency room, where doctors examined her.

They were unable to find a cause for her rapid heart rate, but everything became clear to her in that instant. Suzanne decided that she needed to cut down on coffee. Yet, as time went by, she started drinking it again and wondered how she'd ever stop. She tried drinking decaf, but it wasn't the same—she needed the real stuff. She couldn't understand how she would get through the day without caffeine, and she thought about the holiday season, when her friends always bought her gourmet coffee blends. She didn't want to miss out on any of that!

Suzanne woke up one day tired and drowsy, ready for her morning coffee. Then she noticed that there weren't enough beans to make even half a cup. She fumed! It was raining outside, and going to the store was the last thing she felt like doing. So she started rummaging through the cupboards, but all she could find was some decaf green tea. She normally used it to make an iced tea drink, but thought she would give it a try as a hot beverage.

She started drinking the tea and felt okay. By noon, Suzanne still felt pretty good. She kept drinking the green tea and found that she could think more clearly. She no longer had a fog surrounding her. She also felt guided to increase her water intake and begin exercising regularly.

Today, Suzanne has more real energy than she's had for years. She's more connected to herself and feels wonderful! Recently she told a friend that she'd given up coffee, and this person asked, "What did you do with the 'real' Suzanne?"

Suzanne was pleased to inform her friend that she is now more "real" than she's ever been.

★

Kevin Hunter wanted to detox from something he had been ingesting before he was in his mid-30s. He felt that his angels wanted to clear the energies around him, so he began working very closely with the angelic realm.

They guided him to detox from coffee first. Kevin could feel that coffee was reducing his ability to connect with the Divine world. He noticed a palpable difference when he drank coffee, as its energy would sit in his aura and make his angels harder to hear. Kevin also had a long history of anxiety. His regular coffee drinking was exacerbating this condition and preventing him from achieving peace. The angels urged him to give it up, but Kevin resisted this change, as he disagreed with the angels' guidance.

Kevin wasn't a big coffee drinker—he only had one cup a day, and the rest of the day he enjoyed water. He challenged the angels and explained that other people drank far more coffee than he did. He also did research on coffee, which showed that there were no adverse effects from drinking one cup a day.

Each day Kevin would drag himself out of bed at 7:30 A.M. after a minimum of eight hours' sleep. He would make the perfect cup of coffee using his fancy French press. As he got ready in the morning, he heard his angels say, "You don't need it."

Kevin would grumble and ignore them. He insisted, "Yes, I do need my coffee! Why are you so persistent?" He required concrete proof that he didn't need it anymore.

One day after the angels continued to give Kevin the same message, he'd had enough. He slammed his hands down and offered the angels a compromise. He said that if they felt he didn't need coffee, and *he* thought he did, then they should take away his cravings. He gave them full permission to reduce his cravings for coffee—that was the only solution he could think of. If Kevin had a craving for coffee, there was no stopping him from having it, so unless the angels took away this craving, he was going to keep drinking it. The angels agreed to his request.

The next morning, Kevin woke up and went into the kitchen. Strangely enough, he felt full of energy and found it odd that he didn't crave any coffee. He decided to try going for a full day without it. A month later, Kevin was having one cup of coffee several times a week rather than on a daily basis. Soon he was only drinking it once or twice every couple of weeks, and shortly thereafter, he was completely coffee-free!

After 20 years of daily coffee drinking, Kevin wasn't craving coffee at all. Archangel Michael spent several years with him, clearing toxins and negative people from his life. Now Kevin lives stress-free, peacefully, and is surrounded by warm, loving people.

Healing Methods to Detox from Coffee and Caffeine

Prayer

"Dear God and angels, please release me from the hold caffeine has over me. I no longer want to drink coffee, as I know that it makes my precious body work too hard. I love my body and want to nurture myself. I know that if I continue

drinking coffee, I cannot truly experience peace. Please help me become calm, tranquil, and balanced in all ways. I willingly release all cravings for caffeine into the light. I give you permission to help me now. Thank you."

Dandelion Root "Coffee"

Some individuals find the need to replace their coffee with something else. One option is dandelion coffee, which really isn't coffee at all. It has no caffeine or coffee beans, but rather, dandelion roots that have been roasted. It does produce a dark brew, similar to coffee, but the taste is different. Try a cup and see what you think. Many cafés are stocking dandelion coffee, too. You can order a soy dandelion latte and continue being social with your coffeehouse friends!

Schizandra, or Schisandra (*Schisandra chinensis*)

The herb schisandra cleanses and nurtures your liver and will purge you of the toxins from coffee. This herb is a perfect choice, since it helps your nervous system and balances your mood and mind. It also helps you concentrate and focus. So, this herb detoxes the liver and gives you the energy you need to pursue your cleanse.

Archangel Michael's Spiritual Vacuuming

Michael will release anxious energy from your body. Caffeine causes you to put yourself in unbalanced situations, and when you do so, you can expose yourself to lower energies. By calling upon Archangel Michael, these negative energies will be lifted away.

Archangel Michael will clear your chakras from psychic debris, which will help your energy circulate more freely and enable you to better connect to your passions and motivations.

Archangel Raphael's Addiction Release

Work with Archangel Raphael to sever your cords of addiction. Be willing to let go of coffee and caffeine for your highest good. Raphael can show you the harm it has been causing you, so if you choose to, ask him why you would be better off not consuming caffeine. Without judgment or pressure, the angels will identify the areas of your life that will improve.

7-Day Plan to Detox from Coffee and Caffeine

Day 1

- Mindfully say the "detoxing from coffee and caffeine" prayer when you wake up.

- Remove all traces of coffee from your home. If possible, remove it from your workplace, too. So if you have your own coffee cup or stash of coffee at work, release it.

- Cut your cords of addiction to coffee by working with Archangel Raphael.

- Before you go to bed, take a moment to center yourself and repeat the "detoxing from coffee and caffeine" prayer.

Day 2

- Mindfully say the "detoxing from coffee and caffeine" prayer when you wake up.

- Dandelion coffee is a good alternative to regular coffee. In contrast, choosing decaffeinated coffee isn't a viable option, as many chemicals are used in the process of removing caffeine. Try dandelion coffee with a little organic soy or almond milk and some organic honey.

- As your body releases the addiction to caffeine, you may experience headaches. We don't want to affirm this, as we're praying for a totally comfortable and effortless detox. Yet, we also want to provide you with some guidance in the event this does happen. Rub a drop of lavender essential oil onto your temples and on the back of your neck. This will very quickly take away the tension from headaches.

- Before you go to bed, take a moment to center yourself and repeat the "detoxing from coffee and caffeine" prayer.

Day 3

- Mindfully say the "detoxing from coffee and caffeine" prayer when you wake up.

- Vacuuming with Archangel Michael should be done today. Let go of residues from your chakras, and allow energy to flow through your meridians with ease.

- Drink plenty of good-quality water today. This will hydrate your body and replenish the fluids that coffee has been removing. You'll feel wonderfully refreshed. If you feel tired, reach for some water rather than coffee.

- Before you go to bed, take a moment to center yourself and repeat the "detoxing from coffee and caffeine" prayer.

Day 4

- Mindfully say the "detoxing from coffee and caffeine" prayer when you wake up.

- Clear your mind by taking revitalizing walks through nature. Enjoy being surrounded by trees and wildlife as you let go of the past. Release that which no longer serves you, and move into a new and exciting phase of your health.

- Consider taking a Coenzyme Q_{10} supplement as you detox from coffee. Taking 150 mg per day gives you the spark needed for inspired motivation. Don't fall into a slump as you detox from coffee. Instead, take this opportunity to express your creative desires.

- Before you go to bed, take a moment to center yourself and repeat the "detoxing from coffee and caffeine" prayer.

Day 5

- Mindfully say the "detoxing from coffee and caffeine" prayer when you wake up.

- Start healing your liver by taking schisandra. Take eight drops of the tincture in a little water, three times a day. Schisandra purifies your liver and balances your nervous system and mind.

- Relax by inhaling the fragrance of German chamomile oil. Have it diffused through your home or office in an aromatherapy burner. It won't put you to sleep, but rather, it relaxes your mind so you can focus on what truly matters. Pay close attention to your thoughts, as they are messages from the Divine.

- Before you go to bed, take a moment to center yourself and repeat the "detoxing from coffee and caffeine" prayer.

Day 6

- Mindfully say the "detoxing from coffee and caffeine" prayer when you wake up.

- Place some African violets on your bedside table. These healing flowers will absorb any stress from your day. They will cleanse you of all negativity and leave you feeling refreshed and alive. When you wake up the next morning, you'll feel exhilarated, not exhausted.

- Cleanse your sensitive body withregular sea-salt baths. Take a cleansing bath tonight as you detox your physical body.

- Before you go to bed, take a moment to center yourself and repeat the "detoxing from coffee and caffeine" prayer.

Day 7

- Mindfully say the "detoxing from coffee and caffeine" prayer when you wake up.

- Now that caffeine is out of your system, you can quiet your mind. The angels are easier to connect to, and you will begin to hear their guidance again. Take time for meditation, and make it a part of your regular routine. The more you meditate, the higher your vibration will be. As you rise with newfound energy, you will open up to new experiences from the Divine world.

- Before you go to bed, take a moment to center yourself and repeat the "detoxing from coffee and caffeine" prayer.

You've gone one week without coffee, and now you can see that mornings are a beautiful time of day. As you release coffee, you wake up from the slumber it has held you in. Enjoy your new energy levels, which come from a place of pure joy and good health.

Cigarette Smoking Detox

Cigarette smoke contains more than 4,000 harmful chemicals, which are inhaled with each puff. Out of these, over 70 are said to be cancer causing. Quite literally, every cigarette is doing you damage. Conversely, the opposite is true: every cigarette you don't smoke is improving your health.

Many people rely on cigarettes because they create feelings of relaxation, comfort, and enhanced energy. Sure, nicotine and other stimulating chemicals are present in every inhalation, but in spiritual truth, all positive feelings come from a place of love. God didn't create cigarettes, or guide anyone to do so. These are tools to make you sick and unhealthy so you cannot achieve your life's mission. Cigarettes are as far away from love as you can imagine. Their energy is very low and heavy. However, if you surround yourself with the healing light of the angels, you'll find that you become averse to smoking.

When you smoke at home or in public places, you're also putting others at risk. Secondhand smoke is even more harmful than the firsthand variety. It encompasses all the toxic fumes that the smoker's body instantly rejects.

Your actions are influencing those around you, so please be conscious of the effects of smoking if you have small children or other loved ones around you.

Addictions convince you that you aren't addicted at all. Some people say they only smoke a couple cigarettes a day. Others state they can give them up anytime they like. Yet, they don't and can't. They continue smoking and inhaling toxic fumes.

One day I (Robert) had a patient come to see me for fertility advice. This young lady had been trying to get pregnant and wanted to know if there was anything natural we could do to enhance her fertility. Some of her friends had told her about the treatment I'd given them in this regard, and the success they'd experienced.

As we worked through her case, I wanted to know more about her diet and lifestyle habits. She told me that she smoked four cigarettes a day. This, for her, was no big deal, as it was such a small amount. I, on the other hand, thought differently. I explained the extent of damage that she was doing to her body, and informed her of the impact smoking could have on a newly developing baby. I suggested that we focus on releasing cigarettes first, and then we could work on addressing her fertility issues.

Sadly, she did not share my views and chose to continue smoking. I didn't feel comfortable treating her after that. Our first rule as naturopaths is to do no harm. I couldn't help her get pregnant if her newborn would be exposed to toxic compounds. This little baby would have been surrounded by smoke, even in the womb.

If you smoke, it's your free will to do so; we don't wish to judge or shame anyone. However, we feel strongly that you should be educated fully about what you're doing to your body. Now here's what the angels say about smoking:

Smoking cigarettes creates damage to the third eye and aura. It's the same damage that affects the lungs. Clairvoyantly, it looks like fire burning through plastic. If you know what emphysema looks like, then this is what your aura experiences. It becomes thin and weakened, leaving many openings for negative energies to pass through. It deteriorates the sensitive area of your third eye, making it harder to psychically see.

★

Surrounded by binge drinking and drugs, Melissa Howe didn't like the person she was becoming. She was drinking alcohol every day after work, and she would smoke a pack of cigarettes every few days. Thankfully, she never got into drugs, despite her many friends who used them, but her lifestyle was making her so unhappy and was creating a cycle of abusive relationships.

Melissa decided she'd had enough of this, and her body also started giving her signs to quit. She was having panic attacks and feelings of sadness, and was wheezing so much that it would wake her up at night. Her immune system was depleted, and she was constantly sick with colds and flu. Melissa knew it was time to give up the all-night partying and the smoking and chose her health as her first priority.

So on the December 26, 2005, Melissa gave up drinking for good. A few days later on January 4, 2006, she quit smoking and overhauled her diet—and she's never looked back! She stopped drinking coffee and gave up fast foods, which helped her lose 66 pounds (30 kg).

But when Melissa detoxed, she experienced some challenging symptoms. She had headaches, anxiety, shakes, and more panic attacks, but in spite of these issues, she continued pressing forward. Melissa knew deep down that she had to do it if she wanted to live longer.

In 2011, Melissa attended her first workshop on angels. It helped her face and release her fears and allowed her to detox from the painful emotions she'd stored from the past. By detoxing physically, and now emotionally, Melissa found a new direction and passion. She became motivated to work on her true mission, which was helping children. As a result, she began studying and recently completed a certificate in children's services. Soon she'll get her diploma. She also wants to write spiritual children's books, as her goal is to show kids how to deal with grief and loss by learning about their angels.

Melissa was able to connect to *her* angels and remember her purpose by detoxing her life.

★

Margo Bereska had been highly sensitive to artificial additives and chemicals since childhood. As an adult, she was convinced by her ego that she could eat and drink whatever she wanted. She would suppress her spiritual gifts through alcohol, drugs, and cigarettes.

Over a period of three months, Margo was clearly shown the energetic impact of her diet and lifestyle. She could see the vibrations of the chemicals in her food, and she felt the negative toxins she was ingesting. She knew she had to change this, and felt it was time she listened to her angels.

The angels urged Margo to give up smoking and shocked her by informing her of the huge amount of toxins she was inhaling. They told her that smoking was sucking the life out of her. She began to remember past lives where she associated smoking with a peace ceremony. This is why she felt calm when smoking a cigarette.

Margo was connecting to ancient Egyptian energy. While reflecting on a past life, she could see communication with cats as part of her purpose. This was confusing to her, so she went to her table to have a cigarette. Out of nowhere, a black cat ran into her home, leapt onto the table, and stared her in the eyes. The cat knocked the cigarette right out of Margo's mouth before she even had a chance to light it.

Margo was astounded by the physical presence of her feline angel. She chose to quit smoking at that very moment. And since that day, she has never smoked again.

★

Alexandre Musruck was a heavy smoker who felt as if cigarettes were his best friend. He would refer to them as his "girlfriend," as they were always there to listen to him.

Alexandre had a car accident during which his life was saved by an angel—he received a visit from Archangel Raphael, who helped keep him alive. Shortly after that, Alexandre began to see angels everywhere! His angels helped him detox from chemicals, and guided him to release all unhealthy substances and people from his life.

The angels helped him quit smoking without experiencing any cravings at all. Today, five years later, he often forgets that he used to smoke. He now works as an intuitive counselor, free from the smoke that was polluting his life. He's married and the proud father of two-year-old Raphael!

Healing Methods to Detox from Cigarette Smoking

Prayer

"Dear God and angels, I ask you to surround me with your healing light. Please send me love, compassion, and good health right now. I ask you to repair any damage that smoking has caused me. Please release all of my desires and cravings for cigarettes. I ask that you surround me with supportive, healthy people. I'm ready to make this positive change in my life, and am willing to follow your guidance and trust the direction you give me. I know I'm about to experience greater health, and by detoxing from cigarettes, I'm opening myself up to even greater forms of love. Thank you."

Oat Straw (*Avena sativa*)

Oat straw, or oat green, relaxes the nervous system. This is an important step in breaking the addiction cycle. If you experience cravings, your brain needs time to override them. Most cravings last only moments; with the healing herb oat straw, your nervous system has the ability to think before you act.

Saint-John's-wort (*Hypericum perforatum*)

Saint-John's-wort urges your body to produce more serotonin. This feel-good hormone balances your mood and energy, and interrupts the cycle of addiction by replacing cravings with joy. Studies conducted on Saint-John's-wort have found that it may assist with smoking cessation. One study compared an extract of Saint-John's-wort with a commonly prescribed pharmaceutical drug for quitting smoking, and it was found that a similar number of people successfully quit from both groups. However, when reevaluated some time later, many people from the pharmaceutical-drug group had begun smoking again. The Saint-John's-wort people had quit for good. There's also research being conducted to compare the use of nicotine-replacement skin patches to Saint-John's-wort, and a combination of the two.

Vitamin C

Every cigarette leaches vitamin C out of the body, which causes premature aging of the cells and oxidative damage. It depletes your immune system and makes you more susceptible to infections. Given that the lungs have already been weakened, it's a good idea to take vitamin C. This nutrient rebuilds your adrenal glands, which are responsible for your energy reserves. Smoking makes your body work incredibly hard to fight against the toxins. So, refueling these energy tanks will have a miraculous effect.

B Vitamins

B vitamins are needed for every single thought that goes through your mind. To keep your thoughts light and happy, you need enough of these vitamins.

For every single brain process, you use up B_6, B_9, and B_{12}. Now think about how many thoughts you're having when you feel stressed and anxious. There are too many to count! This high-speed neurotransmitter firing causes you to rapidly become deficient in B vitamins. Unfortunately, as you become deficient, your stress and anxiety also increase. So, if your daily responsibilities require a high degree of focused thought, consider taking B vitamins as part of your self-care routine.

B vitamins are water soluble. This doesn't mean that you mix them with water when you take them, but rather that they dissolve in the water within your body. These nutrients don't get stored in the body, and thus, you need a constant supply.

You can enjoy whole grains and dark, green, and leafy vegetables. If you're feeling overly stressed and fatigued, eating a bowl of spinach may not be enough, though. You might find it helpful to take a B-vitamin supplement or a multivitamin to get you through the rough patches while you embark on a diet rich in the above foods. Then, as your stress levels decline, you may cease the supplement and focus on food choices. However, this doesn't take into account the quality of what you eat. These days, foods are quickly harvested and then stored for longer periods of time. Every minute they're out of the ground, or off the tree, they're losing vital nutrition. A high-quality B-vitamin supplement may be best for your general health and well-being.

When looking for a B-vitamin supplement, search for balance and strength. Several retail products have fabulous marketing, but lack the formulation to be effective. In recent years, there have been scare tactics regarding the safety of large doses of B vitamins. This has attracted a great deal of media attention, yet the research has never been verified.

Here is a comparison of some formulas:

Vitamin	Formula A	Formula B	Formula C	Formula D
B$_1$	100 mg	2.18 mg	75 mg	50 mg
B$_2$	20 mg	3.2 mg	10 mg	50 mg
B$_3$	10 mg	15 mg	100 mg	50 mg
B$_5$	92 mg	10.8 mg	68.7 mg	68.7 mg
B$_6$	50 mg	6 mg	25 mg	41.14 mg
B$_9$ (folic acid)	400 mcg	300 mcg	150 mcg	500 mcg
B$_{12}$	100 mcg	20 mcg	30 mcg	50 mcg

Formulas A and D have high-strength B vitamins, while maintaining a balanced formula. The levels of B vitamins are in proportion to one another and will be readily utilized by the body. Formula B contains minimal amounts of the nutrients, with disproportionate amounts of B$_9$. This formula could potentially create an imbalance with B$_{12}$ due to the respective dosages. Formula C is okay, yet the large amount of B$_3$ may cause hot flashes briefly after taking it. Therefore, as a stress-relieving, well-being promoter, Formulas A and D would be the most suitable.

Hematite Crystals

Hematite crystals can help clear the energy of addiction as well as lift other negative energies from your body. Carry the crystal with you and hold it if you feel cravings. Take a moment to look at the reflective surface. Ask yourself if you're truly craving something else.

Archangel Raphael's Addiction Release

Call upon Archangel Raphael for guidance and support. Work with his addiction-removal technique to detox cigarettes from your energy.

"Archangel Raphael, please release me from cigarettes now. I pray for your help and guidance to let them go. I understand the harmful effects of smoking, and I now choose to be healthy. I know you'll help me with this. Thank you."

7-Day Plan to Detox from Cigarette Smoking

Day 1

- After several deep breaths, say the "detoxing from cigarettes" prayer upon awakening. Use this as your mantra during the day, and call on the angels for extra support. Know that you're always being watched over, and asking for help means that your angels will be right by your side.

- Clear yourself of any cigarettes, old packaging, ashtrays, lighters, matches, or anything else that you associate with smoking.

- Call on Archangel Raphael, and pray that cigarettes be erased from your life as part of his addiction release. You may also be guided to avoid friends who smoke. Follow the messages from Raphael, and know that he has your best interests in mind.

- Before you go to bed, take a moment to quiet your mind and repeat the "detoxing from cigarettes" prayer.

Day 2

- After several deep breaths, say the "detoxing from cigarettes" prayer upon awakening.

- Start taking Saint-John's-wort, as it breaks the pattern of addiction and dependency. It also lifts moods and promotes happiness. Put ten drops of tincture in a little water just before eating. Do this three times a day unless you're on other medications or have other health issues. In that case, speak to your health-care practitioner before starting Saint-John's-wort.

- Carry or wear a hematite crystal. Anytime you think about smoking, hold the crystal in your hand and feel the craving dissipate.

- Before you go to bed, take a moment to quiet your mind and repeat the "detoxing from cigarettes" prayer.

Day 3

- After several deep breaths, say the "detoxing from cigarettes" prayer upon awakening.

- Start taking a good-quality B vitamin today. Read the description of B vitamins formulas to determine if the product you're considering is beneficial.

- Before you go to bed, take a moment to quiet your mind and repeat the "detoxing from cigarettes" prayer.

Day 4

- After several deep breaths, say the "detoxing from cigarettes" prayer upon awakening.

- Oat green relaxes the nerves and helps interrupt the cycle of addiction. You can combine this herb with Saint-John's-wort, or take it by itself. Again, check with your health-care professional first. Put seven drops of tincture in a little water, three times a day. You can take an additional seven drops if you feel a persistent craving. Remember to also call on the angels to help your cravings pass and to give you strength. You've been guided to release smoking from your life in exchange for better health and more happiness.

- Before you go to bed, take a moment to quiet your mind and repeat the "detoxing from cigarettes" prayer.

Day 5

- After several deep breaths, say the "detoxing from cigarettes" prayer upon awakening.

- Vitamin C is lost with every cigarette you smoke, but you can replenish your vitamin C levels by taking 4,000 mg per day in divided doses: 2,000 mg at breakfast, 1,000 mg at lunch, and 1,000 mg at dinner. Take it just before eating, as this helps with absorption and digestion of this vitamin. Use a supplement that has mineral ascorbates, not just ascorbic acid, as these can be too irritating to the stomach. Do this consistently for three months.

- Before you go to bed, take a moment to quiet your mind and repeat the "detoxing from cigarettes" prayer.

Day 6

- After several deep breaths, say the "detoxing from cigarettes" prayer upon awakening.

- Bring fresh magnolia flowers and leaves into your home and office. The dark green leaves absorb toxins from the air and purify your space. They help to cut the cords of addiction from you, as well as those places that you associate with smoking. Peace lilies are also great at cleansing the air. Bring in salt lamps and air purifiers as well.

- Before you go to bed, take a moment to quiet your mind and repeat the "detoxing from cigarettes" prayer.

Day 7

- After several deep breaths, say the "detoxing from cigarettes" prayer upon awakening.

- Enjoy cilantro/coriander in salads, soups, and smoothies. This herb purges heavy metals and toxins from your body that you acquired through smoking. Make it a part of your healthy eating plan from now on.

- Before you go to bed, take a moment to quiet your mind and repeat the "detoxing from cigarettes" prayer.

You've now been smoke-free for seven days. Already your body is healthier than it was last week. Thank God and the angels for this new sense of vitality, and trust that you'll continue on this path.

Detoxing from Other Addictions (Food, Drugs, Medications, etc.)

Please always seek support from a kind and compassionate practitioner. It's far easier to travel the path of light with someone walking beside you. It may seem daunting or frightening as you pull yourself out of the heavy energy of addictions, but know that it's what your Higher Self is asking for. Have faith that there's a reason you're reading this passage. Realize that you're awakening to the idea of detoxing right now.

You can follow any of the steps outlined above for releasing addictions. With Archangel Raphael's help, adapt the healing methods to suit your individual needs. You can also work with the various herbal medicines, crystals, and flowers that are mentioned.

Some drugs can linger in the liver, or in fat cells. It's safer to gently cleanse these from your body over time. If you do this too quickly, you may risk recirculating the built-up toxins, which could make you feel much worse. It's essential to work with someone who will know how to approach this task safely and effectively.

★

Kevin Hunter, a former addict whose coffee detox story appeared earlier in this chapter, believes that most people who are abusing drugs and alcohol are running from something. Usually it involves some kind of emotional trauma and unresolved emotional pain. They use drugs because they don't like how they feel when they *aren't* using.

Kevin grew up in an abusive and volatile home. By the age of 21, he had turned to drugs and alcohol to escape. He was on cocaine, crystal meth, and marijuana. When he wasn't using drugs, he was drinking excessive amounts of alcohol until he blacked out. (When you black out from alcohol, the angels say you're more open to negative entities attaching themselves to you.)

Kevin had always had a strong connection to his angels and had never had a problem hearing guidance from above. His angels provided him with numerous opportunities to hear their messages, but his addictions were preventing him from accepting them.

But it got to the point where he could no longer hide from his guidance by overindulging; it was time to get clean. Kevin worked with his angels to release his cravings for drugs and alcohol, and by the age of 25, he was completely clean.

Today, Kevin is extremely health conscious and fit. He exercises regularly, is strong and independent, and has a clear mind.

People who know him today have no idea of his past addictions. He has worked with the angels to detox his life step-by-step.

★

Victoria Dawn Ward, from Scotland, began releasing her addictions in 2012. She felt lost and exhausted and wanted to release marijuana and prescription medications from her life, as well as deal with an unhappy marriage, foods that caused her discomfort, and overspending.

Victoria reached out to a dear friend, who gave her a spiritual book to read. She learned about putting her faith and trust in God. Victoria prayed for help in letting go of caffeine and marijuana. She was also guided to use other self-help tools such as meditation, drinking lots of water, meridian tapping, taking nutritional supplements, and herbal medicines.

Victoria started off on the right path. However, her relationship was like a roller coaster, taking her up and down. Victoria felt that her husband was putting pressure on her and making her feel depressed. She lost focus and began using marijuana again. She'd told herself that it would help her sleep, but her Higher Self knew that she was poisoning her body with the chemicals in the drugs.

Then, one night Victoria received a phone call from her husband. He was calling from the police station, where they were searching his car for drugs. She got off the phone and picked up a cigarette. At that moment, she felt an almighty thud, followed by a loud voice saying, "Will you wake up?" Frightened, but motivated, Victoria knew she had to quit for good this time.

Victoria came to realize that her husband of 20 years wouldn't change. He wasn't ready to give up the drugs and alcohol that he habitually used. It was up to Victoria to take the first step. She made the difficult decision to leave her marriage so she could achieve balance, and she subsequently found the support of like-minded, spiritual people who helped her through that difficult time.

Now, Victoria can see that she has a higher purpose. She passed her massage qualification test in January 2013, she's lost weight, and she has been feeling more energetic and vital. In fact, her health has improved so much that she's training for charity walks/runs in the summer.

Victoria was able to achieve a happier, healthier life by trusting in God and the angels.

★

Maggie Brown, a nurse and mother of three from the United Kingdom, stopped believing in God in the 1970s. Maggie's youngest baby was just ten months old in 1983 when her husband died suddenly at work. That week she found God again.

She didn't know much about the angels. Up until her 40s, she'd only heard of Archangel Gabriel. So, discovering this entourage of benevolent beings was comforting to her.

Maggie's doctor prescribed antidepressants to help her with her grief. She began taking the medication and soon felt dependent on it. Maggie thought she heard her angels tell her to stop taking the antidepressants, and the same message was repeated and became more persistent each day. She'd tried stopping them in the past but had experienced sweating, dizziness, and painful shudders every few minutes.

The angels kept guiding Maggie to release the medication, so she found support and medical supervision before trying again. This time she had the Heavenly help of her angels, too! She followed her guidance and freed herself of antidepressants without having any side effects.

Maggie gives full credit to the angels for her detox. She feels she wouldn't have been able to do it without them.

★

Aubrey, from Milwaukee, Wisconsin, had always found it challenging to express herself, so she turned to marijuana to bring out her inner voice. At age 16, she began using it to be comfortable with her personality. Her use kept escalating and she became dependent.

Soon, Aubrey could only connect with others if she was high on pot, but the drug blocked her chakras, and her life was a mess. She was attracting terrible jobs, her finances were unbalanced, and her marriage was suffering.

At age 26, she was still smoking pot multiple times a day in order to cope. She felt lost, trapped, and depressed. No one knew how hurt she felt on the inside. Aubrey likened it to standing at the edge of a cliff getting ready to jump: it's a scary place to be and you don't know if you'll survive.

In June 2011, Aubrey and her parents went to Boulder, Colorado, to visit her brother, and that's where she released her addictions. Aubrey went through a nine-day detox while she was in the mountains. It was there that she learned about the angels and prayed for their support. Aubrey went home drug-free, and with a new appreciation for life. She created the perfect job, her finances healed, and her marriage filled up with love.

★

Lori le Blevec had a difficult upbringing. At the age of 17, her parents split up and her dad turned to drugs. Sadly, he took Lori with him down this path. Until the age of 27, she had a cocaine addiction. After many years, Lori realized that she was chasing after love. She was in dysfunctional relationships as a way to receive the love she never got from her father.

When working one day, Lori found a little black bird with a broken wing. It was her angel. She took the little, fragile bird home and cared for it. As she loved the bird, she noticed that her heart was opening. She no longer needed drugs. The bird healed just as Lori did. It flew away and took with it her dependency on cocaine.

She has now purified her body and mind and is attracting loving people on her path.

Prayer

"Dearest God and angels, I call upon you in my time of need. I am done with this unhealthy diet and lifestyle. I can feel how it's affecting my energy and my mind. Please, I ask you from my heart to help me. I know you can heal all things, and I give you permission to overhaul my life. Please surround me with uplifting angels who will guide me in my recovery. Thank you for this healing."

Detox Plan

Repeat the detox prayer as often as you need to. By saying it with heartfelt intention, you call on the power of the angels. They will support you and heal you in any way they can. Work with any of the previously mentioned detox plans and techniques to release whatever it is you're addicted to. Follow your guidance and stick to your plan, consulting with the Divine, as well as with earthly addiction specialists as needed.

★ ★ ★

CHAPTER EIGHT

DETOX YOUR EMOTIONS

Detoxification isn't something that just applies to your physical body. It's healing for you to release old, toxic emotions, too. There's no purpose in holding on to stress, heartache, or unforgiveness. Your body and energy want you to release these heavy vibrations. The angels are right there guiding you along the path of release, so it's time for you to truly let go and surrender to your Higher Self. It's the one true source of your happiness. When you connect to love, and love only, you experience pure joy. You're certainly able to do this. Don't listen to the ego voice that tries to convince you to hold on to negative emotions. It's in your best interests to follow your angels' guidance instead, so please don't delay your happiness any longer.

Detox from Stress

Psychological stress is very real and can be harmful when endured for long periods of time. Stress is defined as anything that causes your body and mind to work harder. It puts undue pressure on you that isn't necessary. A little stress can be healthy and even motivating—it can help you try harder, meet deadlines, and see what you're capable of. However, constant stress uses up vital reserves and depletes you.

Your body goes through metabolic processes to counteract stressful situations, and your brain may trigger the release of adrenaline. Pumping adrenaline through your already-stressed body makes you feel even more anxious. You may experience a sense of panic and feel that there isn't enough time to do things, as adrenaline speeds everything up. When you're in this phase, the ego is giving you false messages, because in truth, you have all the time you need. Remember: time is a human creation. If we removed all the clocks, watches, and timepieces from the world, could we still function? Of course we could! Stress convinces you that you have to hurry up. The more anxious you become, the harder it is to connect with Divine communication, which stems from peace and tranquility.

Along with adrenaline, endorphins are also released that make you feel good. Some individuals become addicted to stress as they ride the waves of adrenaline and endorphins. Your body will also produce cortisol, a steroid hormone that's beneficial in small doses, to return you to balance. Constant stress continually releases cortisol into your bloodstream. This hormone can bulk you up and increase fluid retention, and as a result, you may experience weight gain and fatigue.

Know that your angels can help you alleviate stress and worry, and you'll achieve greater clarity and comfort by doing so.

★

Amanda Dowel discovered the healing benefits of releasing stress and negative people from her life. In the past, Amanda had been working for a very controlling and abusive family business. Thankfully, she was supported by loving lightworkers—she'd made friends with clairvoyants, healers, massage therapists, and nutritionists. These people did their best to keep Amanda safe, serving as her Earth Angels.

Over time, she came to feel drained and stressed, and also noticed an inexplicable mark on her leg. Her very close friend, a healer, suggested that Amanda leave the negative people she was working for. Her healer friend felt they were causing her emotional and mental stress that was affecting her health.

Sadly, this dear friend had ovarian cancer. She told Amanda that when she crossed over, she would come back to support her as an angel. When the friend passed, a nutritionist she'd once known walked back into Amanda's life. This person, too, was receiving the message that Amanda needed to make a move. When she admitted to herself that she was also hearing her angels say the same thing, it frightened her, as she didn't know what to do next. Yet she continued to hear, "You need to move; you *will* move."

Amanda felt that this was her time to heal. She was already practicing yoga but decided to incorporate better nutrition into her regimen as well. She wanted to nurture her mind, body, and soul. This was all the commitment the angels needed. Unknowingly, Amanda had just said to the angels that she was willing to receive their help, so the angels guided her toward greater health.

The first step was to leave the unhealthy family business she worked for. In October 2012, the family asked her to move out. It was upsetting because Amanda didn't want to go, but it was the push she needed to get healthy. She later received visions of past lives with the same family. She remembered them attacking her and thanked the angels for protecting her now.

She had nowhere to go and wondered if she would become homeless. She sat with her nutritionist friend and reviewed potential new homes, but none of them were suitable. Amanda wanted to live somewhere that felt comfortable, so she prayed for a place that would allow her to heal. Almost immediately, she found herself communicating via the Internet with an old friend. He said that she was welcome to move in with him and that everything would be okay. The angels had heard her prayers and had brought her a good friend, too.

Soon after, Amanda noticed that her weight was balancing, she felt better overall, and the spot on her leg was shrinking. When she asked the angels about the mark, they said it was caused by stress. Amanda then realized the incredible impact stress could have on the body. When she released negative people from her life, her healing began almost instantly.

Healing Methods to Detox from Stress

Prayer

"Dear God and angels, please detox me from stress and all its effects. I ask that, starting today, I begin breaking patterns of stress. No longer will I become flustered, anxious, or fearful.

Archangel Haniel, please bring me peace. I ask you to show me how to live a calmer, more graceful life.

Archangel Jophiel, I pray that you surround me with love. As my body and mind absorb your healing, I will feel stress disappear. Please show me the beauty that surrounds me.

Archangel Michael, I ask you to release all negative energies from my life. I know that the brighter my inner light shines, the less my ego can influence me. I call upon your strength and courage to release fearful thoughts.

Archangel Metatron, please restore my life. I ask you to clear my chakra system to balance my energy. I trust in your guidance and will follow your messages. Thank you."

Uplifting Angels

You're always surrounded by angels. Some archangels have specialties that make them extremely helpful for removing stress. You needn't use any special prayers or fancy words to call on the angels; your heartfelt intentions are all that's required. Even as you read their names, you're calling on these angels to be by your side. Remember to give them permission to help you by surrendering the particular situation over to them and God. The request "Please help me" is enough to receive Divine intervention.

Archangel Haniel brings you grace and poise. She helps you remain calm and centered and always act appropriately. She reminds you that there's no benefit to stressing about a situation. After all, what does it get you? It certainly doesn't bring you any closer to your goal. Work with Haniel to instill peace within you. She may urge you to work with the moon, so take a look at the "Full-Moon Blessing" described in Chapter 2. This can calm your energy and connect you to the Divine Source.

Archangel Jophiel surrounds you with soothing pink light. She clears your mind of negative thought patterns and replaces them with loving ones. She ensures that you focus on happy and uplifting solutions to problems. With this attitude, you quickly move out of stress.

Archangel Michael pulls fear-based energies from your aura. He knows that stress is created from a buildup of lower energies. The ego lives in these lower vibrations. Since Michael removes all negative energies from your life, the ego has little room to cause you stress.

Archangel Metatron creates balance in your life. He adjusts your schedule so you have equal time for work, rest, and play. He knows that you do your best work when you're happy, so he relieves stress to create a better outcome for all involved. If you love what you do, then you never have to work a day in your life. Adopt this approach and live it! As you embrace the positive nature of those around you, the angels provide you with endless opportunities.

Archangel Metatron's Sacred Beam of Light

Call on Archangel Metatron to balance all aspects of your life. He will clear your chakras so that you can process energy better. Everything in life requires balance—even the kind act of giving needs balance, so you'll be able to sense when you're giving too much. If you only give but refuse to receive, you create an unequal exchange. Metatron will show you when this occurs.

Archangel Michael's Spiritual Vacuuming

The ego makes stress worse; it tricks you into believing the lies it tells, and makes you more frustrated and overwhelmed. These behaviors don't help you, or your purpose. The ego hides in negative energy; and the more negative energy your body holds, the louder your ego becomes. The opposite is also true: the more positive, loving energy you hold, the louder your angels are. Michael will vacuum your body and aura to remove negativity.

Essential Oils to Relieve Stress

Pure essential oils have deep healing properties that transcend the physical realm. They enter your olfactory (sense of smell) system and have a profound effect on your mind, body, and spirit. Their action is very quick and immediate, so you instantly feel the healing properties of these oils.

It's important to work with high-quality essential oils. Make sure the ones you're using are 100 percent pure and unadulterated. Certain manufacturers may add synthetic fragrances or petrochemicals to "essential oils." Generally you get what you pay for, and many of the higher-quality oils are more expensive. Do your own research and ask lots of questions about the companies and brands in question.

Some oils are too expensive to sell as a 100 percent pure essence, so they may be diluted in jojoba oil. They can include rose and German chamomile. These oils are perfectly acceptable to work with for healing. The jojoba has no fragrance of its own and carries energy perfectly.

If you feel stressed, calming aromas wafting through your home or work space are very healing. Make it part of your daily ritual to fill your home with a beautiful fragrance. At the same time, you're filling your home with loving energy.

Some lovely, calming oils include lavender and German chamomile, which are both very soothing and gently relaxing. They also combine together beautifully!

Aromatherapy Diffuser/Oil Burner

Add four drops each of lavender and chamomile to an aromatherapy diffuser. It could be a diffuser that heats the oil, or one that uses no heat at all. Research suggests that the unheated oils have a better therapeutic effect, as heat can change the chemical structure and vibration.

The oils permeate through the air and dissolve negative blocks that prevent you from attaining a state of peacefulness. The angels want you to be calm, because when you're in this state, you can hear their messages best. Relax and enjoy the beautiful scents.

Aroma Bath

Place four drops of lavender and chamomile into a bathtub filled with warm water. You can purchase dispersing agents (from essential-oil companies) that help the oils mix with water. Try mixing the oils into one fluid ounce of organic vinegar before adding them to your bath. This disperses the oil and is great for your skin.

Consider including healing salts for further detoxification. One cup of Celtic, Atlantic, Himalayan, or Dead Sea salts work well. The minerals and energy of the salts pull out old energy from your physical and etheric bodies. By soaking in a healing salt bath, you can release your fears and concerns. Let go of any blocks that stop you from moving ahead.

Empower your detox bath by holding your palms over the water. Call upon your angels by saying:

"Heavenly angels, please send your loving light into my bath. I ask that I absorb its healing energy. May it bring me calmness and tranquility. I willingly release all stress and tension from my body. Please dissolve any blocks to achieving my highest good. Thank you."

Then, mix the water with your hands to ensure that everything is combined. Soak in this healing bath for at least 15 minutes, longer if you can. Allow your mind to wander and daydream. This is how your angels guide you through the clearing process. As thoughts and emotions come up, release them fully and completely by letting them move through you, to be washed away.

Journaling

Journaling needn't be done in a "Dear Diary" fashion. You can simply write down all the thoughts and feelings you're experiencing right now. Make a list of things, situations, and people you'd like to release. Then, surrender it all to God. You don't need to keep the piece of paper, but may choose to ceremoniously scrunch it up and throw it away. You can also do this on your computer: open up a new document, write your heart out, and then close without saving. No one else needs to see this letter—it's just between you and God. You'll find comfort in writing your concerns down as a way to release them. You no longer have to process them over and over again in your mind.

Herbal Tea

Chamomile tea is known for its calming effects and mild taste. Enjoy several cups during the day when you feel stressed. Try combining chamomile with lavender flowers, which makes a great-tasting, relaxing brew. It's perfect to enjoy all day long. Or, have some in the evening to promote a restful night's sleep.

Herbs work with your body, not against it, so you can enjoy chamomile during the day without worrying about falling asleep. Yet, when you drink it at night, it creates a deep slumber. The angels guide the process to make sure you receive the healing you need.

Try loose-leaf, organic herbal tea as opposed to tea bags. You'll find that the taste is totally different and the energy is much higher. If you have the opportunity, try freshly picked chamomile. A single flower infused in a cup of boiling water is ideal.

Exercise

Movement of your physical body ignites your natural energy reserves. Exercise is a wonderful relaxer and stress reliever. As you exercise, your body releases endorphins that make you feel better. And the more you exercise, the more relaxed you'll feel.

It's important to exercise in ways that make you happy. You might enjoy spending time in nature by hiking. Take adventurous nature walks to detox from the hustle and bustle of modern-day life. Most national parks have trails that you can peacefully, yet briskly, walk on. Rangers will be able to guide you to the paths that are more heart pumping and challenging.

Perhaps you prefer to be surrounded by others when you exercise. Being in a group environment has many advantages. It motivates you to continue pushing yourself as you exercise and also builds team spirit and adds a social element to your training. Why not encourage a friend to join you on morning power walks, or a trip to the gym.

Find a gym with good energy and nice people. It should be a place where you feel safe and encouraged. There's no point joining a gym if it makes you feel self-conscious. Take a few trial classes before deciding to become a paid member. In some gyms, you may find that instructors are taking their classes outdoors to take advantage of the fresh air.

You might choose exercise that doubles as a meditation experience. Yoga is perfect, as it challenges your body and requires your mind to focus. You can indulge in tranquil visualizations while you hold various yoga poses. Pilates is another excellent form of exercise. It involves movements that might look simple, but when repeated, certainly work to build your strength.

The sooner you form an exercise routine, the sooner you'll discover its healing benefits. To really feel the relaxation effects from exercise, you have to work hard enough. Exercise at a moderate pace—it's important to know your limits, but also to know how far you can push yourself.

To ensure the release of mind-boosting endorphins, you need to get to the point of giving up. It's at this point where you'll push yourself a little further and break through that barrier. You might have heard of a "second wind." This is when endorphins get released, so you'll also notice an increase in perspiration as you push past that level. And then when you finish your workout, you'll feel relaxed, flexible, and have a sense of clarity.

Calming Crystals

Connect with crystals that relax your nerves and allow you to focus on peace.

Blue lace agate brings you tranquility. Its pale, sky-blue energy melts away stress and worry. It relieves anxiety, lifts away fears, and focuses on the cause of your stress. Blue lace agate then pulls out this stress through the layers of your aura until it's fully released.

Amethyst dissolves all negative energy and transmutes it back into love. Amethyst is a protective stone, so it's useful to carry around when you're near negative or draining people. It clears away unpleasant or hurtful thoughts, allowing you to focus on love. Amethyst awakens your intuitive abilities, which allows you to clearly know which paths bring you peace and which ones bring about stress. In this state of enlightenment, you can avoid stressful situations.

Citrine calms anxieties and brings about a sense of direction and authority. It anchors your energy within your body, which prevents you from drifting off into negative scenarios. It increases your self-esteem and your confidence and reminds you to enjoy your creativity. By embracing your natural talents, stress naturally disappears.

Fluorite balances your thoughts and emotions and allows you to prioritize the jobs and tasks you need to complete. It organizes your thoughts so that you can better understand where they are coming from. It relaxes you, because you feel confident that everything happens in Divine timing.

Smoky quartz clears the fog of confusion that may surround you. It helps you see the clear path ahead and recognize ego-based thoughts. You're guided and protected by the angels, and smoky quartz will give you extra help by lifting your energy above any chaos.

Peaceful Flowers

The angels of nature bring tranquility and peace into your home. Surround yourself with the flowers listed below and you'll feel their soothing energy. Their healing envelops all aspects of your life. Carry photos of blooms in your wallet or purse for daily support. Put an image of flowers on your computer desktop or screen saver. By doing so, you're constantly reminded of God's love. Flowers show you that you have two options in any situation: do you tackle it alone, or do you ask your angels for help?

These flowers help dissolve stress and infuse peacefulness:

Begonias help you become more patient. They reinforce your personal space and remove distractions from your surroundings.

Daisies ask you to simplify your life. You've taken on too many tasks, so give yourself some needed rest and ask for help. Daisies also advise you to release draining people from your circle of friends.

Fuchsia lifts you up and over this current hurdle. It helps you to continue pressing forward as you move into a stress-free life. Archangels Michael and Metatron work with this flower to balance your schedule.

Gardenias release stress and worry by reminding you to have fun. These flowers are great for long-term stress. Inhaling the delicate perfume of gardenia flowers instantly calms you.

Hibiscus reminds you of the immense support you have, which comes from loved ones and your healing angels. You may not actually "see" those who are helping you; however, the angels ask you to trust that your prayers have been heard. Hibiscus carries the energy of Archangels Chamuel and Raziel. These angels allow you to find the Divine light that shines through any illusion of stress.

Jasmine takes you deeper into your meditation experience. Here you can more easily connect with your angels and the healing energies embracing you. Jasmine is a very peaceful and wise flower to work with. Leave all concerns and worries behind, and receive comfort in your connection to God.

Jonquil affirms that only peaceful people may enter your space. Distance yourself from "friends" who are more interested in receiving favors from you than giving them. Allow this natural transition to occur, and send love to all involved.

Lavender, in all its forms, calms your nerves and relaxes you. It eases tension throughout your body and makes stress a distant memory. Lavender flowers open your third-eye chakra to allow for greater clairvoyance. With this sacred ability, you can see the path to happiness.

Lilacs are connected with Archangel Michael. These flowers combat the fatigue that accompanies a frenetic routine. They're excellent for anxiety and depression caused by a fast-paced life. Each day may seem like an effort rather than a gift. Lilac changes that so you can enjoy the exciting opportunities that await you.

Orange lilies aid you in looking past the small things. They open your eyes to seeing the many miracles around you and pull you out of fear mode, which lets you see yourself for who you truly are.

Yellow roses calm the mind, which allows you to focus on the steps needed to proceed. These flowers awaken a place of peace within you that feels very safe and relaxing. In this space, you release stressful thoughts and concerns.

Tulips help when you feel that you aren't making any progress. Ask that these healing flowers give you the time, space, and whatever else you need to complete the tasks at hand. They remove feelings of annoyance and anger, putting lightness and joy in their place.

Repairing Adrenal Exhaustion

Adrenal exhaustion is becoming more and more common as many people overwork themselves and succumb to stress. Your adrenals are the gas tank for your body and are meant to serve you with a constant energy supply. When the tank runs low, you're guided to fill it up and recharge. However, with so many daily demands, many people forget how important it is to rest. Instead, they push themselves to the limit and empty the tank completely. This leads to a host of health complaints as the adrenals become exhausted.

If you've suffered from long-term stress and have a very demanding life, then read on to see if you may have adrenal fatigue.

As you run out of energy reserves, you'll crave stimulants— you'll want more coffee, caffeinated beverages, and nicotine. Unless you ingest high amounts of stimulants, you might feel that you can't get through the day. You'll feel exhausted, drained, and incapable of planning ahead. The adrenals sit on top of the kidneys and also aid in fluid balance, so those suffering from adrenal exhaustion can crave sweet, sugary foods as well as salty snacks.

Generally, energy levels will be poor. Adrenal fatigue makes it hard to concentrate, and motivation is lost. Interestingly, with the surge of adrenal hormones, people feel more energized in the evening compared to the rest of the day. They retire for the night, lying in bed wide-awake and more alert than they've felt all day. But once they do eventually fall asleep, they may be woken up by uncomfortable night sweats.

To repair your adrenal glands, you need to dedicate yourself to treatment, which isn't something that can be done in a week. You may certainly feel drastic improvements very quickly, but you need to continue for several months for the results to hold. Acknowledge that your motivation is poor right now, but know that if you're committed to helping yourself, you will reap the rewards.

Herbal medicines are so healing when it comes to adrenal exhaustion. There are two key herbs, licorice and rehmannia, that help restore and improve adrenal function. They give you energy until they've healed these important glands. Unlike stimulants such as coffee and cigarettes, these herbal medicines give you energy while rebuilding your tank of fuel. Stimulants give you a false perception of energy and deplete you further.

Licorice (*Glycyrrhiza glabra*) is unlike the type you buy in the candy aisle of the supermarket. This is the root of the licorice plant. Herbal licorice is energizing, restorative, and nourishing to your system. It's also anti-inflammatory, healing to your digestive system, and good for coughs. *A cautionary note:* People with a history of high blood pressure should avoid licorice. Since it impacts the adrenal glands, and their host kidneys, it can elevate blood pressure slightly. This isn't an issue if you've never had high blood pressure before.

Rehmannia (*Rehmannia glutinosa*) is an adrenal restorative herb. It balances stress hormones to treat the source of fatigue. As you become calmer, your adrenals will be under less pressure. Licorice and rehmannia work beautifully together, and you can take both herbs simultaneously for an effective healing result. Take 2 mL or 40 drops of both licorice and rehmannia tinctures, three times per day. Mix with a little water or juice, and drink just after eating.

Healing Financial Concerns

Everyone is abundantly provided for, but your ego will do its best to trick you into having a "lack mentality." It gives you the impression that you have to compete in order to survive, and says there's not enough to go around. It also tells you that you must work incredibly hard to be paid, and that even then, the money you earn will barely cover your bills. It says you have to save for years to take your dream vacation or purchase that perfect home. The angels, on the other hand, say you can have anything you ask for; you just have to be willing to receive.

We're all born with the very same opportunities for success. No one has anything special hidden up their sleeves, and we can have just as much as the people we look up to. At the end of the day, we're all human, and we're all children of God. God doesn't love some of us more than others, and doesn't give extra blessings to a select few. He loves each of his children equally and provides for us all in the same way.

To walk through the day with a sense of poverty is very disempowering, but the angels can shift your view to abundance.

If you feel financially unstable, ask the angels for help. Welcome their assistance without limitation, and trust that they know the best path to follow.

Attached to your soul's energy is a never-ending pot of gold. You're born with abundant energy and can access it at any moment. Some people go through life constantly struggling with their finances. Others choose to see what's inside their sacred soul—treasure—and embrace their abundance.

Some will argue that it's not spiritual to ask for money, but God and the angels want you to be happy. They want to see you with a beaming smile on your face. If financial security brings you that happiness, then the angels will deliver. You needn't feel guilty about asking the angels for financial abundance—they want to give it to you! You aren't taking from someone else—that's the ego's limited way of thinking. There's an unlimited supply for everyone!

Healing Methods to Attract Abundance

Money Exercise

Money is an energy, just like everything else. In the same way that you'd ask God to send you healing energy, ask that money flow toward you. The angels ask you to view money as an energy that you deserve to receive. If you fear abundance or have issues receiving, it's difficult for the angels to deliver it to you.

Think for a moment about your attitudes about money. Many people say, "When I win the lottery, life will be better." If someone were to knock on your front door right now, or approach you in the street with a big bag of cash, what would you do? Would you welcome that abundance into your life? Or would you stand there asking, "What's the catch?" It's the latter attitude that prevents the angels from helping you in this area! Let's delete that old phrase from your vocabulary. Be willing to accept money in any form, from any source.

Try this exercise:

Get a bill in any denomination, and have a pen and piece of paper handy, too. Quietly center yourself and connect to the vibration of money. Hold the bill in your hands, or gently gaze at it.

Next, ask yourself the question: *How do I feel about you?* Write down everything that pops into your head. Even if it seems unrelated, jot it down so you can revise it later. Notice how your body responds, any visions you see, or words that you hear. Write it all down.

Then, ask the question: *How do I treat you?* Again, write down your thoughts, feelings, and visions.

Finally, ask the question: *How can I have more of you?* Listen to the money as it speaks to you.

Learn from this experience so you can alter your outlook in the future. Follow your guidance with respect to how you can have more money and feel comfortable about it. You deserve to be provided for, to be wealthy, and to be successful. The angels know you're happier and healthier if your earthly needs are taken care of.

Universal Check

Creating your own Universal check is a way to affirm your desires to the angels. It doesn't have to look like a regular check, as the phrasing is more important than the appearance. Type up a page that says:

> I, [insert name], *am willing to receive* $[amount] *on or before* [date].

> I give the angels permission to guide me and assist me through each step.

> *Signed,*

> [your signature]

Once it's been printed and signed, place it in an area where you'll see it. Print several copies to place around your home, carry in your wallet or purse, and meditate with. See yourself having the finances that you need.

I (Robert) can attest to the power of this method. I used it when I signed up for Doreen's mediumship class in Hawaii. Back then I was a full-time student with no job, no income, and no passport. By the time I needed it, I had all the money I asked for, and I was able to take a wonderful trip. How did it come to me? I didn't need to know. I just allowed the energy of abundance to manifest without limitation.

Flowers for Abundance

The yellow lily is like a magnet for abundance, as it welcomes all forms of prosperity into your life. Purchase the lilies before all the buds have opened, then sit with these flowers and pour your heart out to them. Send your true intentions into the flower buds by silently praying for help. At the same time, visualize the green energy of money infusing into the lilies. As the buds begin to bloom, your prayers will be released into the Universe.

The Stone of Abundance

Citrine has an energy of attraction that pulls in the things you desire. After cleansing the stone, sit with it and connect to its vibration. Share what you would like with the crystal, and be honest and specific. You might say you'd like a home located in a particular suburb, a car that's a certain model, or a job that makes you feel happy. The crystal isn't going to judge you. The more specific you are, the more the stone can help you.

Affirmations

Positive affirmations are a good way to retrain your thinking, since they build up the energy around you. Then, you can manifest your heart's true desires. Affirmations work best when you say them and also feel them. It's important to believe in what you affirm, so it may take a little while before this becomes a natural process. Please persevere, as you only have wonderful experiences to gain. Repeat your affirmations as often as you like, multiple times a day. Here are some of our favorites that you might wish to use:

- *I attract abundance.*

- *I am willing to receive.*

- *I trust that God and the angels are providing for all my needs.*

- *I welcome money into my life.*

- *I have more than enough money to pay my bills and to have fun.*

Visualization

A visualization is a silent affirmation that allows you to "see," in your mind's eye, how you'll experience your new abundance. With your eyes closed, give yourself the full experience of what you desire. Smell that new-car scent, feel the wooden floors of your new home beneath your feet, or smile as you enjoy your career. Spend five or ten minutes imagining that you've already attained your desire. If you get bothered by negative thoughts, stop and start again. Or, take a break and come back to it later. Do this visualization several times a day, each time adding a new layer to it. Include thoughts, feelings, fragrances, emotions, and anything else you feel guided toward. Following this exercise, you will be guided down the path of abundance. Take this Heavenly message and welcome all that you desire to be Divinely delivered.

Clearing Your Path to Abundance
with Archangel Michael

Archangel Michael clears blocks to receiving. For the angels to deliver abundance to you, you must be willing to accept it. Metaphorically, open all doors and windows. This gives the angels many opportunities to share their blessings with you. Michael gives you courage and strength, and reminds you that it's safe for you to be powerful and have money. Allow Archangel Michael to clear away old belief patterns that connect money to controlling or lonely people. Delete thoughts that say you must be "scrooge-like" in order to become wealthy. Archangel Michael knows your path to success, so let him take the steering wheel and guide you to your heart's desires.

Sit in a quiet space and call upon Michael by saying:

"Archangel Michael, please help me now. I ask you to vacuum away all lower energies connected to money. Please remove all negative thoughts and stress surrounding financial issues. I ask you to open my mind to receiving the gifts of Divine abundance. I trust that you and God will bring me the money I need. Thank you."

Stay in your quiet, contemplative state as Michael suctions away lower energies. By letting go of the fear, you make room for more joy.

Manifesting with Archangel Raziel

Archangel Raziel holds the secrets of the Universe. He knows the contents of your soul's contract, and he also understands profound spiritual laws. He works closely with the Law of Free Will, which teaches that you can have greatness or choose suffering. There's never a reason for you to suffer—always choose happiness, love, and abundance! Work with Raziel to unlock the methods of manifestation that will work perfectly for you.

Dedicate some time to meditating on your hopes and dreams. Light a gold candle and say this prayer:

"Archangel Raziel, please share your spiritual teachings with me. I pray that you show me how to create the life I desire. Please unlock the pathway to abundance so I can be happy and fulfilled in all ways. Thank you."

Allow the information to flow into you like a computer downloading software. You don't need to know *how* it's happening, or even *what* is happening. Just surrender to the healing and let Raziel perform his miracles.

Let the candle safely burn until it runs out. Take time during the candle burning to repeat the prayer and meditation.

Afterward, you'll notice coins appearing on the ground. Pay attention to the dates on those coins, as they can hold significance. Soon the angels will bring you all the financial support you need.

Releasing Painful and Negative Emotions

Your emotions are the first order of priority in your totem pole of health. They can lead your physical body down a path of pain . . . or peace. The thoughts and feelings you experience create your reality, so be sure that you maintain high energy and positive thoughts all day long. If you've suffered from painful experiences, it may be difficult to focus on the light, so know within your soul that darkness is just an illusion. It was created by the ego as a way to prevent you from being happy.

Remember, the happier you are, the more inspiring you become. When you inspire others, they can also join you on the path of happiness. You'll naturally be led to your bliss and to completing your Divine life purpose, but the ego wants you to focus on the pain and hurt you've experienced. But be assured that God and the angels only want you to have joy in your life, so choose to detox your emotions and only allow love to greet you on your journey.

Emotions such as grief and anger are normal human feelings. You needn't judge yourself for experiencing them. The concern comes up when you get stuck. If you become angry and are then laughing again minutes later, that's okay. But if you get angry and are still stewing about those toxic vibrations hours, days, months, or years later, there's an imbalance.

Know that you can safely release these old, stored emotions and make greater room for peace. Allow yourself to acknowledge the journey you've experienced. Understand that nobody is perfect, and that, yes, you may have made mistakes. But this doesn't mean that you've failed at life. You're doing the best you can. The angels ask you to acknowledge your past so you can move forward into the future. Remember to take it step-by-step. You may be guided on a journey of detox if you've been storing old emotions for years. This is something the angels will help you with— they'll let you know when you're ready to try new techniques. To release old emotions, you have to be honest with yourself and with God. Be assured that the Creator is all-loving, so there's no fear of judgment.

A touching example of how the mind can affect one's health is the story of Mr. Thomas. He came to see me (Robert) for treatment for his alopecia, which is a condition that causes the hair to fall out in sections, leaving bald patches on the scalp. Mr. Thomas had a severe case—he'd lost his eyebrows as well as his eyelashes.

He had been brought to the clinic by his girlfriend. She wanted him to seek treatment, but as the consultation progressed, he seemed very resistant to seeing a naturopath. He sat with crossed arms and legs and gave minimal responses to questions. The naturopathic approach to this condition would have focused on zinc supplementation or the immune system. However, as the consultation continued, I asked when all this had begun. Mr. Thomas replied that he'd suffered from alopecia for the last seven years. Around that time he'd gone through a very painful and difficult divorce and had lost custody of his children. As he became very emotional, I realized that those events had caused his complaint! In order for his alopecia to heal, treatment needed to focus on the root of his problems. After he began treatment for his emotional wounds, his hair began to grow back.

Healing Methods to Detox from Painful Emotions

Prayer

"Dear God and angels, help me to heal from these painful emotions. I ask you to lift away the heaviness I've been carrying with me. I'm willing to let go of grief, anger, resentment, unforgiveness, and heartache. I know that you can show me a better way to live. By releasing these low energies, I can experience loving peace. Please send your healing deep within my heart, and protect me from being hurt again. Thank you."

Archangel Michael's Spiritual Vacuuming

Call upon Archangel Michael for clearing. He will whisk away all negative emotions and leave you feeling lighter.

"Archangel Michael, please lift away all lower emotions from me now. Please release negative thoughts from my mind so I can focus on love. I ask that you cleanse me of any toxic emotions I may have unconsciously held on to. Thank you for this clearing."

Healing Salt Bath

The energy of the ocean is deeply purifying. Swim in the sea to clear negative energies from your aura. If you don't have access to the ocean, bring the energy of the sea into your home. Natural salts such as Celtic, Atlantic, Himalayan, and Dead Sea contain all the elements of the ocean. They're unlike table salt, which is refined and processed. These natural salts have the minerals of evaporated seawater, so when you add them to your bath, you've created your very own ocean. By bathing in saltwater, your body is cleansed of negativity. This also has a physical effect by pulling toxins out through your skin.

You can enjoy your healing bath by only adding salt to your bathwater. Or, you can incorporate even more healing energies into a ritual bath.

RITUAL BATH

You'll need:

1 cup of healing salt

White candles

Your favorite incense or aromatherapy oils (Nag Champa incense and lavender oil are nice)

Run a reasonably warm bath. The heat from the water helps your body release tension, toxins, and stress. Light the candles and sense their purifying quality. Next, light your incense and/or diffuse your aromatherapy oils. They invite in the element of air and the healing energy of the angels. You might wish to vocalize your intentions for the bath by saying:

"Angels, I welcome you into this space. Please allow me to release all lower vibrations from my being. Help me to especially release [name your concern]."

Take a few deep breaths to relax yourself. Take hold of the healing salt and imagine a pure white light penetrating it. Visualize the angels sending in white light to the salt. Feel the salt pulsate and tingle within your palms. Trust that it will draw out any toxins from your body, both energetic and physical. When you're ready, throw the salt into the bath.

Soak in the bath for at least 15 minutes. When you're done, pat yourself dry to hold the positive energies in.

Purifying Essential Oils

Work with pure essential oils to dissolve toxic emotions. Purifying oils include orange, lemon, and eucalyptus. Orange boosts your self-confidence and self-esteem. It clears away blocks to attracting loving friendships and relationships. Lemon cleanses your aura and the environment of lower emotions. It picks you up and gives you a fresh outlook on any situation. Eucalyptus washes away the toxic elements of negative experiences and helps you focus on the lessons you've learned, rather than the pain you've suffered.

Try geranium and rose, too. These oils are effective for connecting to your heart center. They have a delicate floral aroma that will soothe your soul.

Allow the oils to diffuse throughout your home, or place a single drop on a tissue. Inhale the perfume during the day to constantly affirm your healing.

Detoxifying Aura Sprays

Misting a purifying spray through your aura and home is instantly uplifting. These products work by dissolving negative energies through positive vibrations. There's nothing that the darkness fears more than the light. These products vary and may contain essential oils, herbal tinctures, or vibrational essences, or be infused by hands-on healing.

Spray them around your aura, morning and night, to cleanse your energy. They will purify you from the emotions of the day. Spray your home or office to dissolve negative energies from other people, or painful conversations.

You can make your own aura spray by filling a spray bottle with natural springwater. Intuitively include select essential oils, vibrational essences, or prayer. Shake it really well and enjoy it!

Flower Therapy to Release Old Emotions

Bring these flowers into your home to promote healing and the release of emotions. They will remove old energies by spreading joy and peace.

Black-eyed Susan helps you release old baggage. You can release the drama of the past and be ready to embrace the future. Work with black-eyed Susan to free yourself from old emotions and heaviness.

Bleeding-heart blossoms clear out old, painful emotions by anchoring you in the light. They create a lightness for the entire situation. These flowers show you the path of peace and remind you of what it feels like to walk peacefully. By letting go of pain and resentment, you'll be illuminated by the loving light of your angels.

Dandelion flowers show you why you're experiencing certain emotions. They help you work through your issues to fully understand their bases. Once you identify the roots of your problems, you can work on clearing them.

Gladiolus raises your energy and increases happiness. It helps you to release low emotions that cause sadness. This flower connects you to your Divine light and asks you to shine your light onto others, so they may also benefit from the gifts you possess.

The magical **hydrangeas** help you adapt to your situation. They're the flowers of transition, assisting you in easily moving from one state of being into another. Work with hydrangeas to journey past your old emotions so that you can move into a state of pure joy.

Iris clears old emotions, leaving your body feeling revitalized. It detoxes you from negativity and urges your body toward health and happiness. True happiness comes from good nutrition and taking excellent care of your physical body.

Nasturtium makes everything lighter and smoother, balances your emotions, and removes complications.

Saint-John's-wort blossoms lift you above confusion, releasing the psychic fog that creates challenges for you. They inspire calmness and clarity by awakening your inner joy. Saint-John's-wort brings back your natural laughter, which really is one of the best medicines. The more you laugh, the more you heal.

Grief

When you lose loved ones, it's normal to grieve for them. This is a perfectly natural part of processing your emotions. Allow yourself an adequate time to heal through the energy of grief.

Archangel Azrael can help you move forward, so call upon her when you feel it's time to leave lower emotions behind. She is the archangel of transitioning from this life into the next, and can help you understand what has happened and how to carry on.

It's important to acknowledge that your loved ones are never lost; they're on the Other Side wishing to communicate with you once again. Know that you still receive loving guidance from those who've passed—you just need to connect in a different way. Obviously, you can't pick up the phone and give them a call or send text messages. But you can feel their Heavenly presence and ask them to give you signs.

Request that they give you messages to let you know they're okay. Next, pay close attention and listen for their names. You may walk past a store where you hear their name called out; you might see it in a newspaper, or hear it on TV. These are all ways they're connecting with you. Trust in their presence and you'll be given more detailed messages with even greater clarity.

If you've been dreaming of your loved ones, then this too is real. They can easily communicate with you when you're sleeping. When you're asleep, the ego is, too, so you don't have an internal battle for the truth. Trust the messages you receive during dream time, and know that they have deep meaning for you.

★

Jacky Walker Kovacs of Sydney, Australia, detoxed her emotions layer by layer. Her detox journey began when she saw a local energy healer. Jacky was guided to see her for anxiety and unexpressed grief following the loss of her husband at age 33. Jacky was left a widow with three children.

After several years, the emotions she suppressed began to surface. The more she received energy healing, the more in touch with her suppressed emotions she became. Jacky had been taught early on not to show or express her vulnerable emotions; she was told she had to be strong and control all that she felt. As a result, she only cried occasionally prior to her healing sessions.

These unresolved emotions eventually caught up with Jacky, and she began experiencing physical symptoms that couldn't be explained. She had physical checkups and was told that everything was in perfect working order, but she could sense that these symptoms stemmed from the unexpressed emotions she'd held on to for years. With the help of her healer, she came to realize that she needed to let go of grief energy.

Jacky saw this energy healer on and off over several years, which helped her connect to deep and personal parts of herself that she never even knew existed. Her medical doctor prescribed anti-anxiety medication and antidepressants as a way to control what was happening, but Jacky's Higher Self knew that these emotions were an important part of her healing. She needed to feel and experience them in order to heal effectively and completely. With professional guidance, she safely stopped taking the medications, but she did continue with her emotional detox in order to process the emotions she needed to feel.

Jacky found the safety of her home an effective place to release the unexpressed feelings, as she'd been holding on to some of these old emotions since she was a child. The energy work slowly peeled away layers of unexpressed feelings, one by one. She realized how much her suppressed emotions had been affecting her energy field. She knew that until she cleared those emotions, she'd just continue to re-create similar experiences.

During one session, Jacky had a profound awakening experience. She felt the unconditional love of God and the angels surrounding her. From this point on, Jacky knew that she was Divinely protected. She felt she no longer needed to visit the healer, yet her soul carried on the healing work. She would feel emotions surface and was guided to experience and express them. Then, she was able to move on to the next unresolved emotion. Jacky noticed a definite difference in her energy and outlook on life as she detoxed her emotions.

Before she began releasing emotions, Jacky was urged to start physically detoxing. She took good care of herself by ensuring that she received adequate nutrition. It appeared that the angels were preparing her for what was to come.

As Jacky detoxed her emotions, she noticed other changes in her life. She became more sensitive and aware of the people and relationships she exposed herself to. As such, she decided that it was to her and her children's benefit that she release certain people from her life. These negative people weren't adding to the health and vitality that Jacky was seeking. The more she detoxed, the more she connected to her true self. Almost simultaneously, she would release the old as she was greeted by the new.

She now spends her time with more compassionate and loving people who naturally flow into her life and provide her with the support and care that she deserves.

Jacky is now in a place where she doesn't judge her emotions. Rather, she chooses to experience them and let them move through her naturally. If she feels grief, she cries. If she feels anger, she expresses it without directing it toward anyone. If fear comes up, she calls on the angels and releases it.

Tuning in to her emotions has been one of the most incredible experiences of Jacky's life. Today she relies on her intuition to guide her daily. The more she detoxed, the clearer the voice of her guidance became. This healing process swept away the voice of fear and gave her soul direction and awakened her own spiritual gifts. Jacky began doing healing work and reading people's auras, just as her healer had helped *her*. As she continues her journey of spiritual discovery, her children benefit from the healing love she's able to share with them.

Grief-Releasing Malachite

Malachite crystals help you move through the stages of grief. They support you and uplift you. Moving forward with your life doesn't mean forgetting those who have passed. You're just choosing to focus on the love and compassion they brought to the world. You acknowledge, but don't dwell on, the sadness of their transition.

Carry malachite crystals with you, and place one over your heart to heal grief energy.

Flower Therapy for Grief

Calla lily is the perfect way to say "I love you" to your soul mate. It sends your heartfelt thoughts in prayers to your loved one. Rest assured that this person will feel your love. In return, you too will connect with this individual's love.

Gladiolus raises you above grief, reminding you of the love that is shared. After communicating with many deceased loved ones, we (Doreen and Robert) can tell you that they prefer to speak of their loving moments. They don't want us to focus on the trying times before they passed. Instead, let's honor their wishes, and their lives, by remembering the joy they brought you.

Surround yourself with **proteas** to clear the energy of grief. This flower helps you find comfort in knowing that your loved ones are still supporting you. They never leave you; you just need to connect with them differently now. This flower helps you maintain healing communications with your departed loved ones.

Anger

Anger is misdirected energy. The angels say it's a sign that there's too much going on with you and that your nervous system can't cope. You can heal this situation by asking others for help.

The angels say that angry people are those doing everything by themselves. They feel that they can't rely on others to get the job done. Their egos make them angry and frustrated because they think they're running out of time. They feel they'll never catch up and that there are too many things to achieve. This brings about great stress to the body and makes them burn through their precious resources faster than they need to.

Relax and find peace, and you'll see that life doesn't have to be hectic. If you've accidentally slipped into a cycle of anger, there's a way out. You can break this pattern by reaching out for support. Simply think *Angels, please help me,* and your healing will have already begun.

You don't have to go through this process alone. Pulling away from Divine help makes your tasks even more challenging. Take a moment now to welcome Heaven into your life. Ask for direction, clarity, and most important, help.

Anger issues can be a symptom of liver dysfunction. If you have indigestion, bloating, difficulty digesting fats, or skin concerns, your liver may need healing.

★

Chrysa Wyland was 30 when she had her fourth child, after which she suffered from postpartum depression. Her doctor prescribed antidepressants and anti-anxiety medications, which she took for years. Later she became obese and turned to drugs and alcohol for comfort.

One day as she was cleaning out her closet, Chrysa got the feeling that she would die young. Initially she was okay with this outcome and thought others would finally notice how wonderful she really was. Then she started thinking, and knew that she had to do something to prevent an early death. She sat down and counted all her blessings and decided in that moment to be happy. So, Chrysa safely weaned herself off medications with her doctor's support. She had no excuse not to feel happy.

She was guided to stop drinking alcohol and taking drugs, and to just get healthy. She got a new job that she enjoyed and started running several miles each day. Chrysa was on top of the world. Her children and her husband were wonderfully happy, and from the outside, everything looked fine. But Chrysa was actually stuffing down old emotions. She didn't want to face them or express them, so she pushed them away and pretended they didn't exist.

Not long after, Chrysa found a lump in her left breast, which was diagnosed as cancer. She was furious. After being the healthiest she'd been in years, how could this have happened? She began a downward spiral, and soon she was eating and drinking anything she wanted. Deep down she knew it was wrong, but she didn't know how to stop. She reverted back to covering up her emotions through eating and drinking.

She went through chemotherapy, radiation, and surgery. Chrysa realized her life was totally unbalanced. She began arguing with her husband, and her children were heading down the wrong path. She didn't realize that her unexpressed anger was making things worse. Then Chrysa received the awful news that the cancer was back.

This time she was ready. She told herself that no matter how painful it was going to be, she was digging up the past. She knew she had to detox from the old energies she was holding on to. She researched how she could heal herself and become healthier. She started eating a plant-based diet; made fresh juices every morning; and released sugar, coffee, and alcohol. She was exercising every day and meditating. Chrysa even sought help from a therapist to fully clear her anger and old emotions.

Once she started praying to God and the angels, her second round of chemotherapy became more bearable. Her side effects were minimal despite the strong treatment. She could feel her body cleansing itself, and it wasn't just physical cleansing, but emotional, too. She was releasing the toxins from her unhealthy diet, and washing away the emotional pain of the past.

Chrysa has a good feeling about her health now. Her family has responded, too, and are mirroring her good health.

Calming Herbal Tea

Calm yourself down by drinking chamomile tea. Have one or two cups a day as the norm, then have another cup if you feel anger start to surface. The process of making tea and sitting down to drink it is enough to deflect the energy of anger.

Relaxing Essential Oil

Enjoy the fragrance of lavender throughout your home. Place seven drops in an aromatherapy oil burner, and allow the scent to remove angry emotions and negative energy, which block your third-eye chakra.

Anger-Releasing Crystals

Connect with amazonite crystals, as they help defuse the anger that may be controlling you. Also use tiger's-eye crystals, as they help you to pause and focus. Stop for a moment instead of jumping from task to task. Carry these crystals in your pocket all day, and place them beside your bedside table in the evening.

Flower Therapy to Detox Anger

Begonias remind you of the importance of patience. When you're patient, the angels guide you along the path of peace. These flowers help you retain your own personal space. Anger can surface when others constantly invade your work area, so by inviting begonias into your environment, you'll be protected from distractions.

Dandelions dissolve angry thoughts and feelings. Enjoy eating dandelion greens in salads to release anger and irritation. These flowers show you the silver lining in your current experience.

Snapdragons clear anger and negativity from your speech and encourage you to use healing words and loving phrases. These words will be of service to others, so by uplifting your vocal vibrations, you can share your healing gifts with those around you. Hold a single flower and then write down your frustrations on a tiny piece of paper. Then fold the paper up very small and pop it inside the snapdragon. Toss the flower into your garden and release the anger with it.

Tulips give you motivation when you feel that you aren't making any progress. They clear anger and annoyance by bringing about peace and relaxation. They help you focus so you can complete the tasks ahead of you.

Resentment

Resentment toward others carries an energy similar to jealousy and bitterness. Holding on to these lower energies is only bringing your own vibration down, and only harms *you*. Ask yourself if you really wish to inflict harm upon others. You know that the answer is *no*. Yet by holding on to resentment, you're wishing harm upon yourself. Be willing to let go of this old energy so you can enjoy life again.

The ego tries to convince you that there's not enough to go around; therefore, you have to fight in order to survive. If someone else has something you want, you'll have to compete to win it back. In spiritual truth, there's more than enough for everyone. You never have to compete to provide for yourself, your family, or your loved ones.

The ego wants you to waste time by trying to take from other people. Your angels remind you that you only need ask for anything your heart desires. Then, your prayer can float up into the Heavens, where God can orchestrate your Divine requests. These requests needn't seem big or grandiose. Rather, your desire may simply amount to getting a parking space easily or driving home in light traffic. By asking, you'll effortlessly get what you want. Now you don't have any reason to slip into stress or to resent those who may have attained what you wish for yourself.

See how simple daily activities can be improved upon? Imagine how relaxed you'll feel when you incorporate this type of thinking into every aspect of your life. No longer will you stress out or feel anger and bitterness toward others. Instead, you'll take the high road, since you'll trust that God is taking care of you.

Healing Dandelion

Dandelion eases resentment and bitterness. There are many ways to work with this herb. Find fresh dandelion in the grass to meditate with. The flowers will lift your lower emotions. If there are seed heads available, you can focus on your wish of peace. Blow with all your might until the seeds float into the sky.

Also, drink dandelion tea. You can find both the leaf, which works closely with the kidneys, and the root, which helps the liver. Both of these teas help flush resentment out of your system. Dandelion herbal extracts and tinctures are also available. Use drop doses to dissolve resentment and jealousy.

Flower Therapy to Detox Resentment

Snapdragons calm you by giving you a moment to think before you speak. When working with these flowers, you'll find more joy in your communications. Let go of the lower energy of resentment, and allow yourself to enjoy spending time with your loved ones. Those people who've caused you feelings of resentment mean you no harm. By working with snapdragons, you will find that there's no need to compete with others or begrudge them what they have. You're just as deserving of a joyful life experience as they are.

Unforgiveness

Unforgiveness is one of the biggest blocks to your spiritual gifts. The energy attached to it is so dense and so low that it pulls you below the frequency of your angels. When you're mired in a state of unforgiveness, you can't hear, see, feel, or know the guidance that God is sending you.

The angels say that by refusing to forgive, you're only hurting our own Divine light. Your inner light is more beautiful than you can imagine. It glows with a high vibrancy that shines like a lighthouse in the dark. Your soul's light can never be extinguished, but when you hold on to unforgiveness, you place a blanket of darkness over that light. It's still shining, but now it has become harder to connect with. The angels also describe unforgiveness as a dam in a river that halts the flow of your body's healing energy.

The process of forgiveness is simple, but the journey to accepting it can be challenging. When forgiving someone, you choose to release negative energy that has attached itself to you. You aren't saying that what the other person did to you is okay; you're just forgiving the perpetrator to free yourself. You are choosing to release the pain and the power this other person has had over you. It's now time to reclaim your strength and affirm your peaceful future.

Depending on your healing journey, this concept may be difficult to understand right now, so try not to let your ego distract you, and don't let it draw your focus away from this book. The ego wants you to hold on to low energies as it prevents you from forgiving others.

When you help yourself and rise above darkness, you'll see that we're all Divinely connected and come from the same Source. Our essence, our soul, comes from the same loving Creator. When connecting to this concept, visualize the other person as a small, innocent baby. When you do so, the process of forgiving becomes easier.

The angels ask you this question, "Would you rather exchange your pain for peace?" Repeat the affirmation:

"I am willing to exchange my pain for peace as I forgive."

Say this to yourself to dissolve blocks to receiving your angelic healing.

Forgiveness Meditation

Quiet your mind by focusing on breathing with very deep, slow inhalations and exhalations. Count to four as you breathe in. Then breathe out on a count of four. Continue this breath work for several minutes. Once you feel sufficiently relaxed and centered, call upon your angels:

"Angels, please be here with me. I ask you to bring me your healing energies and guidance."

Feel their calming presence around you. Next, visualize yourself in a safe, private area. You might imagine a mountaintop, a peaceful river, or a warm and inviting beach. See your angels with you in your mind's eye. They're here to protect and support you during this release.

Now, invite the person you're willing to forgive to join you in this safe space. Sense his or her energy meeting you in calmness. This is your opportunity to say everything your mind and body has been holding on to. Express yourself fully to the other person, knowing that it's safe for you to do so. If you feel emotions surface, allow them to do so. Release them as part of your healing. You might also ask the other person questions. Wait patiently for a response. You'll receive it as feelings, words, visions, or thoughts. This individual's energy will be giving you the answer. You can ask your angels to help you understand what's being said, and they can help you release pain arising from the answers you might receive. When this visualization is complete, call the angels to your side. Visualize them sending healing energy to both of you. Next, say:

"I am willing to release you from my life as I choose to forgive."

You'll instantly feel dense, lower energy leaving your body. Thank the angels for their beautiful support, and trust that the clearing has taken place.

Be gentle with yourself for the remainder of the day. Take a nap if you need to. Let yourself rest, and follow your body's messages with respect to food and drink.

Heartache and Disappointment

Heartache and disappointment leave scars on your energetic body. Clairvoyantly, we see these scars sitting just above your physical body. They show that you've been hurt, or burned, in the past. It's important to clear these old wounds to prevent these patterns from repeating themselves. A painful relationship breakup can leave unresolved heartache in your energy field, which makes it challenging to begin a new relationship. You'll continue to meet the same partners, who seem to disguise themselves in different bodies. Their energy feels the same, though. There was a reason your past relationships dissolved, so please don't put yourself through these painful experiences again. Work with the angels to release these old energies and embrace positive changes and new relationships.

★

Naomi Sirio, from Australia, had been having difficulty in her marriage for several years, but she felt that she'd recovered from the trauma of her husband having an affair four years prior. Deep down, Naomi suspected that his infidelities had spanned their entire 25-year relationship, but she convinced herself that staying in the marriage was best for her children.

However, Naomi was getting physical signs that she needed to detox from emotional pain. She started having lung infections, liver problems, and gynecological pain. She prayed to the angels to give her signs, but she ignored the ones she received.

After much thought, Naomi chose to leave the relationship. This was a difficult decision to make, but one she knew was needed.

As Christmas approached, she saw that an Angel Visions workshop was going to be held in Sydney. For the first time in 25 years, Naomi was able to purchase a ticket without being ridiculed. It felt so liberating just to buy the ticket!

Naomi received the guidance to start a physical detox to accompany her emotional clearing. She received a detox diet plan from a dear friend and embarked on her journey. She started to detox a week before the Angel Visions workshop. The angels asked her to release coffee, and she received the tools she needed to do so.

After just one week, Naomi noticed a significant change in her energy. Previously she'd let fear run her life. Now, she felt calm, in control, and safe. The angels also orchestrated it so that Naomi would be chosen by us (Doreen and Robert) for a flower reading! Naomi now trusts the guidance she receives from the angels and continues to improve her life.

Healing Heartache with Archangel Raphael

Raphael heals your emotions and removes heartache. Work with him to clear negative experiences from the past. Your soul carries a canvas with it, which has imprints of previous relationships, disappointment, and heartache. Work with Raphael to wipe the slate clean and welcome change.

Begin by meditating on your breath. Next, call on Raphael by saying:

"Archangel Raphael, please bring your loving, healing energy to me now."

A slight change in air pressure or tingling is a sign of Raphael's presence. Or, you may just get a sense that he's with you.

Next, visualize a canvas that displays your hurtful life experiences. Usually the canvas will appear as a jumbled-up mess with many overlapping pictures. It might look like scribbles, or appear as if paint has been splashed all over it. Ask Raphael to remove these old hurts by saying:

"Archangel Raphael, please wash away the old energies held on this canvas. Please allow me to easily and effortlessly release painful memories from the past. I ask you to heal me so that I never have to endure the same hurtful experiences again."

Be aware as Archangel Raphael sprays the canvas with his healing, cleansing fluid. Feel old emotions leaving your body and being released into the light. The paint and color will drip away, revealing the pure white light underneath. Raphael now asks you which images you'd like to see on the canvas. Allow yourself to attract your goals and desires.

Thank Archangel Raphael by saying:

"Thank you, Raphael, for this powerful clearing. Please continue working with me so I can attract and affirm a positive future."

Heart-Healing Quartz

Rose quartz crystals gently reintroduce love into your life. They dissolve blocks by helping you attract loving, compassionate people. Then you can let your defenses down and welcome others in. These crystals help you see that not everyone is bad or trying to hurt you. Many people want to see you succeed and share in your Divine happiness and light.

Flower Therapy to Detox from Heartache and Disappointment

Gladiolus pulls you out of sadness and heartache. You have a great deal of love and light to share with the world, and God needs you to be in perfect condition. Holding on to old energies of heartache blocks the messages of love from your angels. Let go of these blockages and let the love of God back into your life. God and the angels have never left your side, but due to your recent circumstances, you haven't listened to them. Now is the perfect opportunity to reconnect, and share your deepest emotions with your loving guides.

★ ★ ★

CHAPTER NINE

DETOX YOUR ENERGY

As a sensitive person, you unknowingly absorb other people's energies. These energies—especially toxic negative ones—can affect your physical and emotional health. In this chapter, we'll look at ways in which you can clear your personal energy and the energy in your home and environment. . . and keep it clear.

Clearing Your Home Energetically

Every day you probably spend a great deal of time at home. Whether you're awake or asleep, you're in the same environment, so your home should serve as your sanctuary—a place where you can let go of the cares and concerns of the day. It should be a place where you can find peace and happiness. Even if you share your home with others, you deserve to feel comfortable in your surroundings. Most important, your home should be a place to relax.

Just like people, your home has an energy. You've most likely walked into someone's home for the first time and felt instantly at peace. You can sense that the people who live there are filled with love. You feel safe letting your guard down and being authentic with them.

Conversely, you may have gone to someone's home and felt uneasy. The energy is poor, which makes you anxious and nervous. It might be difficult talking to others, or you find yourself engaging in unusual behaviors. Take note of these experiences, because they give clear messages about the energy of your environments.

Of course, this doesn't mean that a home with negative energies has nasty residents living there. They may be very loving and kind, yet the energy of the home will dim their kindness and trigger negative responses.

Think for a moment about *your* home. How do you think total strangers would perceive it? Would they say it feels very comfortable, or would they feel anxious?

Think of what you learned about crystals in Chapter 1. Even if you haven't worked with them for a while, they still appreciate being cleansed. They absorb lower energies just by being around you. Well, your home can do the same—think of it as a sensitive object that will also absorb the energies it's exposed to.

When others come to visit you, or your children have friends over, you're bringing different energies into your home, and they might not mix well with the energy that's already there. You may be totally focused on loving and helping others, yet your visitors may be materialistic and shallow. As such, their energy will leave a "psychic stain" on the walls.

Arguments and misunderstandings leave energetic imprints on your home, and performing stressful business tasks at home can also leave behind negative energy.

If your home has negative energies, you'll find it difficult to enjoy being there. You may start silly little arguments for no reason, or you might lose your motivation and just watch TV all day. Or, your diet might suffer because you're only eating processed and/or takeout food.

The solution isn't to refuse anyone entry into your home. You can still enjoy the company of your friends, arrange playdates for your kids, and get some work done there. What you need to do is clear your home of these negative vibrations. If you're sensitive, you'll feel when your home needs clearing. If you aren't yet confident in being able to sense this, schedule a house clearing every month. Then, if there are harsh energies present in the interim, you can do another clearing to balance the energy.

★

Michael Soo, an Australian naturopath and Bowen therapist, wanted a simpler, more authentic life; and his Higher Self knew he needed a change. He was surrounded by toxic energy that prevented him from living his potential. Michael started to recognize what was truly important. It wasn't materialistic items such as expensive homes or the latest clothes. It wasn't even about eating at the right restaurants. For Michael, it was about simplicity.

Unsure if it was Archangel Chamuel guiding him or his dearly departed father, Michael decided he wanted to move. He left his suburban apartment in Sydney and traveled to the beautiful and lush Hunter Valley. There, he felt his detox begin. The heavy energies that once surrounded him had no place there. He cleansed unnecessary, toxic influences from his life and released dramatic, stress-inducing people from his circle of friends. Michael chose to focus on family, true friends, and being a part of his community. He's still on his journey, but he knows he never has to look back.

★

Sahitha Yelamanchili was raised in a family home that lacked boundaries and respect. To protect herself and heal those around her, she began working with the angels.

She started noticing the interactions between various family members; and she became aware of how she reacted, and the reactions of others, to the situations. An example is when her aunt would become loud and aggressive. Sahitha would shrink inside and feel awful, yet her cousins would ignore it, or smile and leave the room. Sahitha wanted to change the way these things affected her.

She started to work closely with Archangel Michael. Anytime there was a heated argument, she instantly called Michael to her side. She would ask him to vacuum the area and release the toxic energy. She visualized all tension being dissolved in the home and being replaced with peace. Sahitha asked the angels to shower everyone involved in golden light.

With repeated practice, she's gained confidence. Now when her aunt yells, she doesn't absorb the attack. The last time this occurred, Sahitha actually laughed and thought her aunt's comments were absurd. Thanks to Archangel Michael, she no longer feels frightened.

Chakra Clearing Meditation

My (Doreen's) *Chakra Clearing* CD/MP3 was channeled with the energy of Archangel Michael. It has a deep purifying effect that removes all negative energy. You can play this meditation at home for a clearing. You don't need to sit and meditate with it if you don't want to. Instead, play it in the main living area of your home. It will energetically work like a bug bomb. The positive vibrations of Archangel Michael will permeate throughout your home, dissolving any traces of darkness.

Angelic Clearing

The angels are pure, loving light, and they have a very high energy and vibration. They're able to illuminate the darkest of places, so invite the angels into your home to clear all the rooms at once. For this clearing, you can work with Archangels Michael and Metatron. Michael comes through strongly to remove all negative energy, and Metatron brings balance as he clears the space using sacred symbols.

Sit down in the main living area of your home. Begin by focusing on your breathing. Take long, slow breaths all the way in, and all the way out. Repeat this deep breathing for several minutes. When you feel relaxed, call upon the angels by saying:

*"Heavenly angels, please grace me with your
Divine presence. Please bring your cleansing
light into my home and remove all darkness. I ask
that everyone who resides here feel your purification. May everyone be balanced, and attuned
to the high vibration of love.*

*I welcome in Archangel Michael. Michael,
please enter every room of my home and fill it
with your light. Please remove any negative
energies or fear that may be present.*

*Archangel Metatron, I pray for your assistance,
too. Please infuse my walls with your sacred
symbols. May they bring balance to my home
so that anyone who enters here does so with
peace. Thank you, angels, for creating
a sacred space within my home."*

Now visualize the angels spreading their cleansing light throughout your home. See them dusting the shelves, vacuuming the floors, and washing the windows. See them invoking loving energies to balance your living space. In your mind's eye, follow them through each room. You may notice that they spend extra time in some rooms over others. This may mean that there's heavier energy there or that the negativity has been there for many years. Follow your intuitive feelings about where that energy came from. This will help you protect yourself in the future.

Enjoy your beautifully tranquil home, which now has perfectly balanced energy.

White Sage

Sage has long been revered for its cleansing properties. Traditionally it was used by Native Americans to remove negative energies. This sacred herb, held in high esteem as a gift from the Creator, was used to remove lower vibrations that may have been responsible for illness, loss of vitality, and pain.

White sage has a high vibration that dissolves fear energy, and it's most commonly used as incense for clearing. White sage is available in several forms, loose leaves being the purest type. You can burn these leaves on a charcoal block designed for incense. Your local metaphysical store will be able to help you with this.

Carry the bowl of smoldering herbs around your home. Use your free hand to waft the smoke around. Wave it over crystals, oracle cards, and other spiritual items. Spend extra time around doorways, especially the front and back doors of your home. Cleanse the energy here to affirm that only loving energies may enter. Go with your inner guidance, and trust how long to stay in each room. At the same time, visualize a crystal-white light penetrating the room. Sense the cleansing taking place, and notice how the energy becomes lighter.

You can also purchase smudge sticks, which are easy-to-use bundles of sage that you can carry. Once lit, the smudge stick will continue to smoke. When the smudging is complete, extinguish the stick in sand. This method is more mobile, as you can wave it around like a wand. It's easy to get in and around small objects and cupboards with a smudge stick.

Incense cones and sticks are available, too. Check to make sure the incense is made of real white sage. Some sticks will have a fragrance of white sage but no raw herb. The best clearing effect comes from using the actual herb.

Please also think of the source of your sage. Choose companies and brands that work ethically. It's rare for white sage to be cultivated, so a lot of the herb being used for incense is taken from the wild. If companies aren't mindful, the sage could be stripped bare from an area. Manufacturers need to work with Mother Nature, who ensures that there's enough for next year's crop to grow. You can ask companies for this information or check online.

White Rose

The white rose is deeply cleansing. It's connected to Archangels Michael, Metatron, and Raphael, three of the most powerful clearing angels. It's no wonder that this flower is able to lift the energy of your home. White rose brings about a sense of peace, so allow it to work with your own energy as it performs its purifying work. It may guide you to let go of certain foods, drinks, or friends as you raise your vibration.

Meditate on the purity of the petals, which is the energy this flower ushers in. It clears negativity in all forms, including earthbound spirits—entities that are irritating and negative. The white rose lightens your home and casts away all darkness.

Place a vase of roses in your living room. Very soon you'll notice a palpable difference in the environment. You can also place a single white rose in each room of your home. Now the individual roses will work together as a grid of light. They connect with one another and send healing, detoxifying energies through their etheric network. Leave the roses in place until they wilt. Now you may find that these flowers fade faster than normal. This is because they're being of service. They're giving themselves in exchange for your upliftment. The angels say that we mustn't feel bad or guilty about this process. The flowers want to help you. And, by welcoming them into your life, you're allowing them to perform their sacred purpose.

Flower-Petal Clearing

I (Robert) discovered this clearing method when I was teaching a Chakra Healing workshop. The angels guided me to work with fresh rose petals to cleanse crystals. They said that the high energy of the flower petals removed lower vibrations. The petals infused the crystals with intense love, so I purchased a whole bag of them to use in the class. We cleansed the crystals and then used them to clear our chakras.

Everyone loved this exercise! It brought so much happiness and joy to the room. I thanked the angels for sharing this new and uplifting method with us.

I still had a bag of rose petals that I didn't want to go to waste, so I asked the angels, "How can I make good use of these?" The angels replied that we could toss them all over the ground. They said this would cleanse the room, and our energies, during meditation. So I sprinkled fresh rose petals on the floor. The energy was absolutely magical! The delicate perfume of the roses opened our hearts and purified our surroundings. The space felt (and smelled) beautiful afterward.

Try clearing your home by tossing fresh rose petals throughout. Your local florist may allow you to purchase bags of petals. In my experience, the petals haven't cost very much in comparison to buying roses. I suspect that they're the flowers that aren't "perfect" for the florist to use in arrangements. They can still be very uplifting and cleansing in the right hands. You could even buy fresh roses and ceremonially pluck the petals as you enter each room.

Four-Element Clearing

This exercise incorporates all four elements: *earth, air, fire,* and *water.* You'll work with each of these energies as you move throughout your home. They bring their own unique vibrations in order to dissolve fear.

First, you'll need a representation of each element:

- Earth = salt
- Air = incense
- Fire = candle
- Water = small bowl of water

Place all four items on a table in front of you. Hold your hands slightly above them and visualize a pure white light clearing each item. Then say:

"I ask that the angels please join me and guide me during this home clearing. Please purify my representations of the four elements so that I may use them for clearing. I ask that today we work for the highest good of all."

Continue to visualize white light. Now take the incense and light it. Wave it around your home and ask for the smoke to cleanse by saying:

"With this incense, I ask the element of air, and the angels, to cleanse my home."

Repeat this prayer as you move throughout your home. When complete, return the incense to a safe place and pick up the candle. Take the candle through each room while repeating:

"With this candle, I ask the element of fire, and the angels, to cleanse my home."

When complete, return the candle to a safe place and get the water. Sprinkle small amounts of water around each room. Repeat:

"With this water, I ask the element of water, and the angels, to cleanse my home."

Return the water to the table and then pick up the salt. Sprinkle pinches of salt on the ground as you say:

"With this salt, I ask the element of earth, and the angels, to cleanse my home."

When you're finished, pause for a moment and close your eyes. Feel the purifying energies swirling around you as they release any built-up negativity. Thank the elements and the angels, expressing your gratitude for a balanced home.

Let the incense and candle burn all the way through. Vacuum or sweep the floor, and dispose of the trash in a garbage can outside.

Singing Bowls

Singing bowls clear the energy of a room through sounds. The frequencies of the bowls eliminate negative energies and induce meditation. You can get crystal and Tibetan singing bowls to help you connect to the angels and clear your ear chakras. The crystal bowls are made of clear quartz, or may be blended with other minerals. They have a very pure tone and magnify your intentions. The Tibetan bowls are usually hand beaten by Buddhist monks. Both types of bowls can be used for clearing and healing.

Carry your singing bowl into the room you wish to cleanse. Take a moment to quietly center yourself and focus on your breathing. Set your intention for clearing the space of negativity. Tap the bowl with your playing tool, and slowly begin striking the rim of the bowl. A sound will soon be heard as the bowl starts to sing to you. Let its Divine voice spread throughout the room. Keep playing as long as you feel guided. You'll feel yourself drift into meditation as you play. The frequencies of the bowl trigger your relaxation response and awaken your intuition. You may feel guided to play the bowl in different ways, allowing the sound to naturally stop. Then, strike the bowl again to hear its pulsating voice. Let your creativity flow as you clear the room. You might be guided to move to a particular corner where there's heavier energy. Trust it, and play the bowl there.

When you feel that the room is done, you can move to another. Remember to center yourself first, and set your intention before you begin playing.

Positive Affirmations

Your home absorbs the energy it's exposed to, so make a conscious effort to infuse it with loving thoughts and prayers. You can use affirmations that anchor in positive energy. These refresh the energy of your home as you say them out loud. They're helpful in between clearing exercises, as they instill your positive intentions.

Think of the energy your words are putting into the walls. You'll often hear people say they'd like to paint their home because they want to give the house a new, fresh feel. Sometimes when they complete the task, the house feels heavier than it did to start with. Why? It's likely that the people painting were complaining the entire time. They might have uttered negative things such as "I hate painting," "This is boring," or "This is too much work." These negative phrases seep into the walls and create a dense energy. If you know you dislike painting, or whatever task needs to be done in your home, hire someone else (with positive energy) to do it for you. Otherwise, make sure you use happy and loving words as you perform this job. Visualize the wonderful feel it will give your home.

Here are some thoughtful affirmations to use in your home:

- *My home loves me, and I love my home.*
- *I cherish the feeling my home gives me.*
- *My home is a haven where I can relax and be myself.*
- *I welcome positive people into my home and ask all others to leave.*
- *I feel safe in my home.*

Clearing Yourself

If you absorb lower energies, it's more difficult to be positive and inspiring. The angels say that procrastination is a clue that your body is holding on to energetic toxins. When you procrastinate, you're delaying your happiness—and there's no reason you should ever wait to experience your bliss. Procrastination makes you avoid your purpose by diverting you with meaningless distractions. Online social media can perpetuate this type of procrastination. You might check your e-mail or text messages even though you just did so only moments ago.

The ego says that you need to take care of basic tasks first. Then you can start the ones that truly matter. In this case, you must be strong to acknowledge that procrastination is taking place. Regular clearing exercises and meditation prevent you from falling into this pattern.

You need to take excellent care of your energetic body, as it's just as important as taking care of your physical one.

★

Anita Chakraburtty, an astrologer and naturopath, cleared out her life to find spirituality and her purpose.

Anita was born into a working-class, mixed-race family in the United Kingdom. Her ambition in life was to have lots of money—she wanted the opportunity to buy things without thinking twice. By the age of 30, she was Head of Risk for a large bank. This career made her wealthier than all of her peers, and to others, she appeared to be a success. She owned a big house in London, took five-star vacations, and wore designer clothes. Yet Anita wasn't fulfilled.

Each night she would self-medicate with marijuana. The next morning she would rouse herself from her drug-induced stupor by drinking multiple espressos. Everyone looked at her lifestyle and told her that she'd made it, but she felt unhappy and had no idea why.

She happened to come across a book on Zen Buddhism. This kick-started her search for meaning. She started absorbing information from spiritual books, as she tried to fill the void within her. Deep down she knew that to find true happiness she needed to detox from her job at the bank and her eight-year relationship, and then begin her quest. She traveled to India, Australia, and the South Pacific seeking meaning.

Her search didn't satisfy her restlessness, so Anita returned to her London home. Shortly afterward, she was headhunted by an Australian bank. She decided to leave her friends and family and move to Sydney. It was there that she had her true awakening. On a trip to Uluru (Ayers Rock), her constant mind chatter was replaced by pure silence. She felt a profoundly meaningful connection to land, sky, and Spirit.

She prayed to find her true life's purpose and patiently waited until her path began to reveal itself. Synchronistically, a friend talked to her about getting a naturopathy degree. Her heart opened with joy because Anita knew she could help people in a way that mattered. Her boss at the Australian bank allowed her to work part-time so she could study. Her soul pulled her toward astrology, and she then went on to meet her shaman and is now walking the path with him.

Anita loves her new life—and herself. She is truly happy being of service to others as she nurtures her Divine soul.

Clearing Your Aura

Your sensitive body is affected by the energies it's exposed to. Surround yourself with loving, high-energy people and you'll feel fantastic. If you're around negative, complaining individuals, you'll feel drained and tired. Your body responds to these changes in energy and gives you very clear signs of how it's being affected. Pay close attention to how you *feel* around other people. This indicates whether they'll support you in your life's purpose or if they'll hinder you.

Aura Sprays and Vibrational Essences

Aura sprays make it very easy to clear your energy. They contain detoxifying energies and pure essential oils. They're misted around your aura to purify it, and as they gently fall onto your body, they dissolve lower energies. Spray them four or five times above your head, and inhale the soothing scent.

You can use aura sprays to clear the energy of rooms, too. Mist them throughout your home to purify the space.

Vibrational essences are liquids that cleanse and balance. They're made from the energy of flowers, crystals, nature, and angels. You take them orally by placing a few drops under your tongue. This area connects to your subconscious brain and clears away fear-based thoughts. They can be a useful support during the day and are easy to carry with you and discreet to take.

Making Your Own Detoxifying Aura Spray

There are many sprays available on the market, but unless you know the integrity of the company making it, you may be unsure of the quality. Some manufacturers won't tell you what ingredients they use, which makes it challenging if you're hypersensitive.

Creating your own aura spray is a beautiful process. Follow intuitive guidance from the angels during every step. Choose an essential oil that resonates with you, and find something you enjoy the scent of and that feels good energetically. Each essential oil will have its own specific properties, but for the purpose of this exercise, the angels ask you to choose one intuitively. Next, ask the angels how many drops you should add to your spray. Trust the first number you get. Then, add that specific number of drops to your spray bottle. Fill with springwater and shake vigorously. You may need to shake the bottle for a good five minutes to thoroughly blend the oil with the water.

Now place the spray in front of you, with your hands softly around it. Call upon the angels and God, and ask that they create a clearing spray by saying:

"Dear God and angels, please transform this into a deeply purifying aura spray. May it cleanse all negative energies."

Visualize pure white light coming from your palms and into the spray. Feel the detoxifying nature of the liquid. Trust that it will clear the energy of anything it touches. Infuse it with Archangel Michael's royal blue light for additional clearing properties.

Now enjoy using your spray!

White Sage

Use this incense to clear the energy of your aura. Stand over the smoldering herb to receive its clearing. Or, you can have a fellow lightworker clear you by wafting the smoke over your body.

Purifying Shower of Light

The angels will try to give you simple guidance that you can follow. They will ask you to clear your energy fields daily and give you easy ways to do so. The angels say you can program the showerhead in your bathtub with purifying light. So, as you perform your daily ritual of showering, you will receive an energy clearing, too.

Rub your hands together to awaken the palm chakras. Separate them and hold your hands over the showerhead. Imagine golden light coming from your hands and storing itself in the showerhead. Invite the angels to help you by saying:

"Angels, please infuse my showerhead with purifying and detoxifying light. Every time I bathe beneath this shower, my energy will be cleared. I will leave feeling refreshed, reenergized, and motivated. Thank you."

Visualize golden light, coming from the angels and your palms, being absorbed into the showerhead. The next time you shower, take a moment to affirm the shower of light by mentally calling on the angels. This simple step ensures that your energetic clearing takes place.

Healing Salt Bath

A detoxifying bath can be Heavenly after a stressful day. It washes your aura through the cleansing properties of the ocean. The angels say that healing salt baths pulls toxins out of your physical and energetic bodies. Enjoy soaking in a purifying bath to awaken your Divine spirit.

Archangel Michael's Cord Cutting

Archangel Michael says that every time we interact with people and help them, we form a cord. These cords are based in fear and serve no benefit or purpose. If they're allowed to stay in your auric field, you'll become drained, fatigued, and may experience inexplicable pain.

Cut your cords daily with the assistance of Michael. (See Chapter 1.) Make it a habit to call on him to clear your energy. Connect the idea of cord cutting to another daily routine such as brushing your teeth or shaving. During these activities, call on Archangel Michael and sever your cords of fear.

Crystals to Dissolve Negativity

Any crystal will have uplifting and clearing effects on your energy. Some healing stones are excellent to carry daily, so follow your gut feelings as to which ones you're drawn to, as they'll serve as healing tools for you. You may not know their specific healing properties at this moment, but trust that they're calling to you for a reason. Later you may look up the metaphysical properties of your crystal, or you can intuit your own meaning given the situation you're in right now.

Amethyst has the ability to transmute lower energies into positive vibrations. It works on all levels of your being. It even takes away negative thought patterns that manifest in your aura. Carry amethyst crystals in your pocket, or wear them as jewelry for detoxification.

Flower Therapy Aura Clearing

Flowers are one of the highest-energy parts of a plant, and carry the imprints of the angels and fairies with them. This high vibration and purity is excellent for removing negative energies from your aura. Work with a white rose for cleansing and purification, or use your intuition to choose the right flower. Ask your angels for guidance before visiting your local florist.

Once you have your chosen flower, begin slowly moving it through your aura. Work with it like a wand to comb out old vibrations. Intuitively wave the flower over particular areas of your body. You may feel guided to hold it a little longer over your head area if your thinking has been foggy. If you've had back pain, you might be urged to keep the flower over your back for a while.

Be mindful of these feelings, and know that the flower and the angels are working with you. They're helping you understand where your body is storing lower energies. Once you identify this, you'll be able to prevent it from occurring in the future.

Anticipate how your body processes energies to understand the messages it's sending you. You'll realize that back pain may be a buildup of negativity rather than something with a medical cause. In cases like these, taking pain medication won't have any effect. The source of the pain isn't physical.

Shielding

Once your aura is sparkling like new, you'll want to keep it that way. Spend time strengthening your aura and shielding it. It would be a perfect world if there wasn't the need for shielding.

However, not everyone has the same loving outlook on life that you have. Therefore, it's best if you practice shielding, especially before going to crowded places or spiritual events.

Some people think that shielding is a way of anticipating attack. They feel it's an affirmation to the Universe to send the energy of attack toward you. When we asked the angels, they said that it was just like locking your front door. If you leave the door open, you're allowing anyone and anything to enter. By closing that passage, you have access to the little peephole on the door to determine who gains entry. You get to decide which vibrations can enter and which ones stay outside.

Your particular situation will determine how often you need to invoke your shield. A general guideline is to practice this twice daily: once in the morning when you get up, then again in the evening as you go to bed. Most shields will last for approximately 12 hours. However, when exposed to harsh energy, your shield may weaken faster than normal. When surrounded by negative people or difficult situations, reinforce your shield every hour if needed. Ask the angels to give you clear signs that you need to shield again. They may give you physical sensations, or the thought of shielding may pop into your mind. Take a moment to shield, and notice the difference it makes in your day.

Angel Cocoon

Visualize a stream of miniature angels gliding down from Heaven. As these little angels get closer, they begin to spiral around you. They start at the top of your head and float around your body—both front and back. They continue all the way down to the base of your feet.

The stream of angels never ends, which makes this shielding exercise so powerful. As the angels come close to you, they pick up and release negativity. They take this low energy away and are replaced by a new angel.

The angel cocoon is very cleansing and comforting. Often you'll hear giggling and laugher, in addition to the sound of wings.

Amethyst Cave

Imagine that you're sitting inside a giant amethyst cave. You're surrounded by protective purple light that the crystal emits. Every crystal point is absorbing lower energies from your body and aura and is detoxing you from heaviness and pain. Once they've removed all darkness, the crystal points infuse your body with healing. The amethyst cave awakens your intuitive abilities and strengthens your connection to the angels. This is an excellent meditation to do prior to visiting metaphysical fairs or giving speeches of a spiritual nature.

Rubber Ball

Archangel Michael stands over you holding a bowl of liquid rubber that's cooling and protective. The rubber deflects any negativity or psychic attack, causing it to bounce off like a ball. The shield is the same color as Michael's aura, which is royal blue. Ask Michael to shield you by saying:

"Archangel Michael, please encase me in a protective shield of rubber. Infuse this rubber ball with your sacred light. May any negativity bounce off, and all love be absorbed. Thank you."

Visualize Archangel Michael carefully pouring the royal-blue rubber over your aura. It will instantly envelop you in protection.

Mirror Ball

See yourself standing inside a mirror ball, just like those at a disco. This shield deflects any negativity or destructive thoughts that others may send your way. It's perfect when you have meetings with others who may not have the best intentions.

Lead Shield

This shield invokes thick, impenetrable lead into your aura. The lead is lightweight, so it's easy to carry around. Visualize metal being infused into your auric field, which will give you an extremely strong defense. This shield is best used when you feel frightened or unsafe. Put it up as you walk home from work or catch late-night public transportation. People will sense your strength and leave you alone.

Colors

Each color has its own vibration, and you can intuitively choose a color to blanket your aura with. Close your eyes—the first color that comes to your mind is the right one for this moment. Tomorrow you may be guided to a totally different color, or the very same one. Trust this inner sense of knowing, and visualize your aura glowing with that hue.

Here are just a few of our favorites to shield with:

- **White**—a strong, pure energy of protection and clearing

- **Purple**—excellent for psychic protection

- **Pink**—protecting yourself and coming from a place of love

- **Golden**—healing energy as well as protective

- **Green**—healing shield

- **Yellow**—great for study and concentration

Detox Negative People from Your Life

Dramatic, draining, and stressful people have no place in your life, as they're merely hindering your good work. You're taking excellent care of yourself, physically and spiritually, but negative people can dampen your light. They overstep boundaries and expect too much from you. Sometimes these people are placed on your path to teach you a lesson, or you may be there to help *them* heal. However, you're not interacting with them so that you can *live* their lives, too. You have your own destiny, and stepping into the shoes of someone else is not it. God and the angels have far greater plans for you.

You might find it helpful to assess your friendships and honestly examine them. A two-way exchange of energy and love is what you strive for. If you're not getting that, certain relationships may need to end.

Sit down and think of a friend. Now ask yourself this question: *If he or she called me at 2 A.M. with a flat tire, would I get out of bed and help?* You might answer yes, as you would do anything to assist a friend in need. But then ask yourself a more pressing question: *Would your friend do the same for you?* Honestly answer this question. (Your Higher Self and the angels already know the truth.) You might conclude that this person would screen your call, make an excuse, or just say it's too late to get out of bed. This shows the true nature of the relationship: it's one-sided and unhealthy.

If you continue putting energy into this relationship, it will lead to burnout. You'll deplete your energy reserves and begin to resent helping people in any way. You never want to get to that point, so it's important to protect yourself from these situations. Speak with a truly compassionate friend who will give you another perspective on the energy exchange. This person will let you know if you're giving too much.

Releasing these unbalanced relationships is the healthiest thing you can do. While it can feel frightening or painful, you owe it to yourself to be happy. Trust in the support of your angels and allow this exchange to end. Occasionally, but not always, when you make this decision, the friendship will heal. The other person becomes more respectful of your time and energy and starts approaching your friendship with a new, more balanced outlook. However, if things remain the same, you'll only be hurt, so choose happiness over drama.

Boundaries and Respect

As a compassionate, openhearted soul, you want to give. It's in your nature to care for others and ensure their health and happiness. Occasionally others may take advantage of your kind gestures and may use and abuse your offer of help. This is why it's so important to enforce boundaries.

It may feel uncomfortable for you to put rules into effect. It might feel like you're placing conditions on how you'll help people, but if you refuse to do so, you'll deplete your own energy reserves. By setting boundaries, you're not saying you don't want to help or that you don't love someone—it's about acknowledging a basic Universal law: karma needs to balanced. The flow of energy on both the giving and receiving ends needs to be equal.

Imagine small children who aren't allowed to play near the road. This is to protect them and keep them safe. If the kids wander out onto the street, they need to be told that it's unsafe. If, instead, they're not told anything, they'll continue to explore a dangerous place. The boundary needs to be put in place so the children understand.

We lightworkers need to take a similar approach with our friends, family members, and clients. We need to honor our personal time and make sure our needs are provided for. If boundaries aren't in place, people can take advantage of us.

It all boils down to respect. If the people in your life truly care about you, they'll respect your decision. Know that it's okay to say no when you need to.

I (Robert) learned this lesson in a rather jarring way. When I first began my healing work, I was offering my services free of charge because I simply wanted to help people. If they were benefiting from our interaction, I was receiving all that I needed. At the time, I was seeing people in my home and soon built up a regular clientele who enjoyed coming to see me. All I was asking in return was a thank-you. However, over time I started to notice that I was no longer even getting *that.*

People began calling my home at 6 P.M. on a Sunday asking for healing. They'd arrive for an hour session and not leave until much later. The angels explained to me that the boundaries were too blurred. I was being taken advantage of because I was allowing it. So I meditated with the angels and asked for their help. They said that I should begin charging a fee. The energy exchange needed to be balanced, and money is just another form of energy.

I was very uncomfortable with this guidance and resisted this advice. I pleaded with the angels to find another solution, but they were adamant. The angels had never advised me incorrectly in the past, so I had to surrender to the moment and trust them.

I asked them what I should charge, and to my surprise, they let me decide. I asked them if even charging $5 would be enough. The angels said that $5 was enough for the boundary to be set, so I informed all of my clients.

To my absolute shock, none of my previous clients came back. This was heartbreaking to discover. Those people didn't even value the session at a paltry $5. Meanwhile, I was pouring my heart and soul into my work. The angels got their message through loud and clear.

If we let people take advantage of us, and if we give "too much," people don't respect the healing that takes place. I thanked the angels for helping me place boundaries around my consultations.

Archangel Michael's Cord Cutting

If you'd like to "cut the cord" between you and another, know that this cord is based in fear energy and serves neither of you. It's sucking vitality from you to the other person and acts as a courier for negative energy to tumble down. So release the negative parts of this relationship, and accept love as Michael cuts your cords.

Sit down in a quiet space. Focus on the friend in question. Remember that you can only sever the cords of fear. You can never—nor would you want to—cut the cords of love, so you're still allowing loving exchanges to occur between you. This leaves the doors open for the relationship to balance and become harmonious. Call on Archangel Michael by saying:

"Archangel Michael, I call upon your Heavenly support right now. Please help me to objectively view my friendships and be honest about them. Help me see when I'm being taken advantage of. Allow me to attract beautiful, loving, caring souls into my life. It's these people I wish to spend my time with. I ask you now to please sever any cords of fear I have with my friends. Please help me release any unhealthy relationships with these people, as you see fit. I trust that you and God know what's best for me. I trust your guidance and listen to your messages. Thank you."

Let yourself release the unhealthy people from your life, and send them love.

Interestingly enough, the people attached to the cords may try to contact you. As you release the negative relationships, others may subconsciously try to latch back on. Be cautious if they suddenly call or text you. Don't be afraid that they might know you released them. They will be unaware and unoffended; however, their egos may try to continue abusing your kind and caring nature. Don't let this continue any longer, as you deserve harmoniously balanced relationships.

Friendship Flowers

Gerbera is the friendship flower, and it attracts like-minded people into your life. These people will love you for who you are and not what you have. Your ego may try to convince you that you're measured by the material items you own. If you have a fast car, an expensive purse, or a big house, then you must be a better person, right? In spiritual truth, none of these things matter. Yes, they can bring you pleasure, but they shouldn't run your life. You don't want friends whom you have to keep up with or compete over. You want people in your life who love you even if you have very little. These are your true friends.

It's important to be with like-minded individuals with whom you can travel on your healing journey. Welcome people with similar views into your life. You can share your healing experiences and angel messages with them!

Bring joyful bunches of gerberas into your home; they will attract the perfect people into your life. Keep a small vase of these happy flowers on your desk at work. This will create a field of mutual respect with your co-workers.

What Qualities Do You Want in a Friend?

Make a specific prayer to your angels to bring you the ideal friends. Make a list of all the qualities these friends must have. Also, create a list of those things you can't handle and that you don't want them to possess. Be sure to include this phrase at the bottom of your list: *Angels, I ask for this or something even better.* You may not be able to imagine the absolute perfect people to include in your circle of friends right now, but trust that God and the angels know the right individuals for you. They will guide you to people who are kind and respectful.

The angels say that this is a good exercise for all of us to do. It tells God what would make us happier. They liken it to people hoping for the perfect Christmas gift. They might desire a new bracelet, yet never tell anyone they want it. They don't express how delighted it would make them to own it. So when Christmas morning arrives, they're disappointed not to receive their ideal present. By sharing their desire with others, they would have had a greater chance to receive what makes them happy. (In truth, we know the bracelet wouldn't equate to happiness, but the love exchanged with giving it, would.)

Releasing Bullies with Love

Enduring the stress and fear of being bullied is devastating to your self-esteem. The angels will help you regain your inner strength and confidence in this area.

Bullies can appear in different forms: they can abuse and attack, and then there are the more subtle bullies who manipulate you. They convince you to do things that, in your heart of hearts, you know you don't want to do.

If your children are being bullied, you may feel helpless. You're unable to watch over them every second during their school day to protect them. You want this to stop but may be unsure what to do. So ask Archangel Michael to be with your children on your behalf. Visualize this strong, protective angel walking side by side with your kids. See them smiling, happy, and most important, safe.

Black Pepper

Black peppercorns have protective properties that eliminate negativity. If someone has been bothering you or your loved ones, use black pepper to clear him or her out of your life. Know that you won't be influencing anyone's free will—you can't force others to do something they don't want to do. The energy of black pepper simply plants a seed that says they may find greater happiness somewhere else. And if they leave you alone as a result, that's a bonus!

Write down the name of the bully on a piece of paper. Sprinkle the paper with black peppercorns and fold it up. With the peppercorns folded inside, hold the paper and say:

"I pray for help now! Please help me feel safe, confident, and protected. The person whose name I've written down here has been causing me pain. I no longer want to feel that this person controls me or my situation. I know that in truth, I am in charge. I allow God and the angels to enter my life and bring me balance and harmony. I send everyone involved love, as I ask for change for the highest good of all."

Now toss the paper into a fire, or set a match to it. As the paper burns, your prayer will reach Heaven.

Detoxing from Technology

As I (Robert) sit here writing, my Internet/phone lines have lost their connection. I just went into panic mode, as I'm so reliant on the Internet. I need it for e-mail, research, checking my appointment calendar (which is hosted online), and monitoring social media. I use the phone for consultations and to return queries.

Without these "taken for granted" luxuries, I feel instantly lost. How am I going to get anything done? It's a scary moment. But just as I start to panic, the angels jump in and say that we *all* need to detox from technology from time to time.

Have you shut down your computer, only to pick up your smartphone to check the internet moments later? In today's world, we've become so reliant on gadgets to help us through our day. Don't get me wrong—I love the technological advances that we continue to have access to, but our bodies (and minds) can do well by taking a break from it all.

As such, Doreen and I have decided to include a section here on detoxing from technology.

A Technological Fast

You've probably heard of fasting with regard to food, but what about doing so with respect to technology? You may try just one item to begin with, since doing without all forms of electronics might prove to be daunting.

A great place to start is with TV, which often features low-energy information that promotes fear. You'll always see news about negative occurrences taking precedence over uplifting success stories. These "heavy" stories lower your vibration and affect your sleep patterns, too. This dense energy sits in your aura and continues affecting you long after you've turned the TV off. A great many television programs deal with frightening situations featuring violence, swearing, and arguing, but you wouldn't stand for this in your daily life, would you? So why would you want to expose yourself to it each day when you turn on the TV? Instead, watch fun, heartwarming programs that uplift you.

Better still, avoid television for one whole week. Note whether you perceive the world differently. Notice if you sleep better. See if you have heightened energy and more positive interactions with others. If so, these positive benefits will urge you to limit your exposure to television in the future.

Try detoxing from other forms of technology, such as computers, phones, and the Internet. Avoid one or all of them for an entire day, or try to go without for a whole week. Ask your angels what you would do best to avoid, and trust your inner wisdom.

Also, try not to use credit or debit cards for one full day. If you're planning to go shopping, withdraw cash instead of relying on your cards. You might see that you spend more cautiously, as using actual money makes you think twice before purchasing items. (Naturally, be safe when carrying cash—keep it hidden, and avoid carrying too much at one time.)

★

Nicole Goodfellow detoxed her home from violent video games. In the summer of 2010, her teenage stepchildren came to live with her full-time. Quickly she realized that they were playing very violence-filled, dark video games. Nicole didn't want to say anything because she wasn't their birth mother. This was a new living arrangement, and she didn't want to damage her relationship with the children.

Being a highly sensitive person, Nicole couldn't tolerate the violence in her home. Her angels continually urged her to remove the video games. She spoke with the children's father, but he resisted doing anything.

Nicole noticed that the children's behavior was changing. These games were taking them to dark places and affecting their schoolwork. She felt that the energy of the house had become violent and heavy. At the same time, Nicole was hearing about violent outbursts on the news that were linked to playing such games. Again, her angels nudged her, but there was little she could do.

Eventually their father put time limits on how long they could play. This didn't work, as the teens found ways to hide their video-game addiction. They were able to bypass the parental-control software and stay up all night playing. When Nicole discovered this, she had no choice but to inform her husband. This was the final straw that led to the detox of all video games in their home.

Strict rules were enforced, and computer use was monitored. Six months later, the children were more uplifted and positive—they'd detoxed from the harsh energy of the video games. Nicole's husband noticed the improvements as well, and thanked his wife for loving the children so much. The entire home shifted energetically and started to fill up with loving light.

Electromagnetic Frequencies (EMF)

Electronic devices emit a magnetic field, which is also known as electromagnetic radiation. Most people are constantly surrounded by electromagnetic frequencies (EMFs). They come from computers, cordless phones, televisions, and even the electrical wiring in walls. They're being sent out by telephone lines and towers.

EMFs can negatively impact sensitive people, who may feel sluggish or lethargic after working on a computer. If you're one of these individuals, you may experience headaches and insomnia. Your body has its own EMF, as does the earth. Not surprisingly, your body is calmed and relaxed by connecting to the electromagnetic resonance of the planet.

Spend quality time outdoors, and connect with nature. It's especially important for children who've been labeled with ADHD. The natural energy of the earth will help balance them.

We've become reliant on the tools that emit EMFs. The reality is that many of us need technology to complete our work, so just be sure that you protect yourself against the electromagnetic radiation, as it's nearly impossible to avoid.

Several items have been found to defuse the magnetic field caused by electronics. You can place these near your electronic devices or wear them on your body. Do an internet search for EMF protection, and research the products you find. Some of them will have scientific support behind them that shows their efficacy.

Go with your gut feelings and let the angels guide you. The angels suggest salt lamps and crystals emit negative ions into the air that purify your living and working environments. Also, they say that any crystal will combat the EMFs through *piezoelectricity*. Crystals have their own magnetic field that reduces the harmful effects of technological EMFs. Even though little research has been done with respect to these methods, the angels ask you to try them. Place a salt lamp in your office and watch the healing effects, and put a crystal right beside your computer. See how much longer you can work without becoming tired.

CHAPTER TEN

DETOX YOUR HOME

Let's take a look at some common toxins found in the home. As we've seen, fluoride is present in tap water and toothpaste. It claims to help prevent tooth decay, yet research shows that it makes little difference. Geographic locations that haven't fluoridated their water have the same rate of cavities as areas that do. By drinking fluoridated water, you can overload your body with this toxin. It can mimic symptoms of arthritis and give you joint aches and pains. It will also cloud your mind and make concentration harder, and it affects children and young adults even more than older people.

Make your own chemical-free toothpaste from organic coconut oil, food-grade peppermint oil, and pure baking soda. Choose natural springwater as your drink of choice, or invest in reverse-osmosis filtration.

Triclosan is a highly toxic ingredient in antibacterial products, toothpaste, cosmetics, and many liquid soaps. It's a synthetic antibacterial agent that is very dangerous. It's been linked with immune- and endocrine-system issues and can disrupt your thyroid function (the thyroid is responsible for your metabolism and growth). Studies have shown that triclosan can increase cell growth and cause elevated activity in the brain. It disrupts hormones in the body and also affects your muscles.

Researchers from the University of California, Davis, and the University of Colorado presented a scientific paper in the *Proceedings of the National Academy of Sciences* that showed that triclosan impairs muscles of the body and heart. They suggested that triclosan forms a very real risk to humans.

Many researchers say that the presence of triclosan has little benefit in antimicrobial and antibacterial hand washes. The process of rinsing your hands and rubbing them together dislodges bacteria and viruses, and the presence of triclosan doesn't make a significant difference. A study was completed on the effectiveness of triclosan as an antibacterial hand wash, and the lead researcher admitted that it's only effective in uncommon situations when there are extremely high levels of bacteria. He also admitted that the research was shaped and funded by the American Cleaning Institute, a trade association for producers of cleaning products. Naturally, they have the most to gain from keeping this harmful chemical in their products.

Phthalates are common in plastic packaging, plastic wrap, and plastic bags. They can also be found in soap, shampoo, hair spray, and nail polish. They're added to plastics to make them stronger and more flexible. Cosmetic manufacturers use phthalates to prolong the scent of fragrances. Phthalates have been linked to reproductive and endocrine-system issues.

As we've touched upon at several points, BPA plastics are present in many food and drink containers. There has been much research done into the dangers of BPA-containing plastics: they leach this dangerous toxin into foods and lead to liver disturbances, heart disease, and reproductive concerns. BPA plastics have recycling number 3 or 7. Avoid these plastics at all costs.

Sodium lauryl sulfate is responsible for the foaming of many hand and body washes, facial cleansers, and shampoos. It may cause allergic reactions with repeated use. It can also damage the protective layer of the skin, which keeps harmful chemicals out. However, with respect to shampoo, there are a number of products now labeled "sulfate-free," so you might want to be on the lookout for them.

Essential Oils as Household Cleaners

You can save money (and save your life) by using pure essential oils instead of the expensive, toxic products sold in stores.

Essential oils can be powerful disinfectants and are provided to us by nature. The oils offer physical cleaning properties along with metaphysical healing energies. This makes them the perfect choice for spiritually aware people like you. An excellent antiseptic oil is lavender. Add lavender oil to a spray bottle of water, shake well, and let sit for several hours. When you're ready to use it, shake vigorously again before spraying the surfaces you wish to clean. After you finish, mist some more lavender over the surface for extra protection. The aroma of lavender is very soothing and helps calm anxieties and fears. It works to open your third-eye chakra and awakens your clairvoyance.

There are many wonderful natural products that you can use for cleaning and self-care. Most of these are common household items. Learn how they can be used in different ways to help you avoid chemical-laden products.

Tea Tree Oil

As discussed earlier in the book, tea tree oil is an excellent antibacterial, antifungal, and antiseptic essential oil. It's perfect for cleaning and disinfecting, as it breaks through bacterial defenses.

Tea tree oil can be used in a whole host of ways. Dab a drop on acne and it will clear up the spots. Pop a few drops in an aromatherapy diffuser to combat colds and flu. Add a little to shampoo to prevent head lice. Use it as an all-purpose cleaner by adding two teaspoons to two cups of water. Put this in a spray bottle and shake very well. Use it on kitchen countertops, in the shower, and to combat mold. If you don't care for the smell, add some geranium oil to the mixture.

Baking Soda

Baking soda, or sodium bicarbonate, is a wonderful household item that's safe for you and your family to use. Baking soda balances the pH of anything it interacts with. Mix a teaspoon of baking soda in a glass of water. Rinse it in your mouth, swish it around, and then spit into the sink. Your breath will be fresh, as the baking soda neutralizes odor and balances your oral health. You can use it as an exfoliant, as it's gentle enough for daily use.

Make a paste by adding a little water to some baking soda. Then, gently rub in circular motions over the neck and face. You can give yourself a whole-body scrub, too! This is also a great hand cleanser for stubborn dirt or odors.

As a natural deodorant, baking soda can be lightly applied to your underarms. Just use the dry powder and pat away any excess. It can be used to neutralize other odors, too. Keep an open box in the refrigerator to absorb odor. After a month or two, dispose of the box by pouring it down the drain. As you do so, let the warm water run from the spigot. It will remove any drain smells and make your sink fresh. Also, you can sprinkle some baking soda in the bottom of trash cans to avoid unwelcome smells.

Use baking soda to clean your home. Sprinkle some onto a damp sponge and scrub the shower and bathroom as normal. Then, rinse off and wipe dry. The tiles will sparkle like new, and there isn't any need to wear a face mask since there are no harsh chemicals!

For baked-on food, sprinkle a few spoons of baking soda into the pan. Add a little water and let it soak. You'll find that food sponges off much easier. Clean your oven by making a paste with baking soda. Apply it to stubborn areas and then let it sit overnight. In the morning, use a wet sponge to clean the inside of the oven. Remove any debris and go over it again with a damp sponge. Mop your floors with a solution of a half cup baking soda in a bucket of warm water. Dust over the carpet and leave overnight. The next day, vacuum up the baking soda for a fresh-smelling room.

Raw (or Virgin) Coconut Oil

Use additional natural skin-care items such as virgin coconut oil. Your skin readily absorbs this natural oil and repairs connective tissue. It can help to minimize fine lines and bring a youthful glow to your complexion. Apply the oil to your face and all over your body.

You can use organic virgin coconut oil in cooking, too. Unlike other oils, it won't go rancid or form unhealthy trans fats when heated. You can use coconut oil to cook at high temperatures and it still remains nutritious. Your body easily digests this oil, which can help you lose weight. As you replace other oils with natural coconut oil, you'll find that you have energy, which will speed up your metabolism.

Nontoxic Insect Repellents

Don't spray toxic insecticides in your home. Instead, create your own blend of natural, safe insect repellent. Add 10 drops of citronella essential oil, 5 drops of lavender oil, and 5 drops of geranium to a 3 fl. oz. (100 mL) spray bottle. Fill with water and shake well. Spray throughout your outdoor areas to naturally repel bugs and insects. You can spray this mixture on your skin, or make a lovely oil to use topically. Make a base of organic cold-pressed extra-virgin olive oil, or organic coconut oil, and add the same essential-oil combination. Apply a small amount to your palms and then gently massage into your skin. You'll smell great, nourish your skin, and keep insects away.

Use peppermint tea as a natural insect repellent as well. Brew a strong pot of peppermint in a closed vessel like a teapot, adding three teaspoons of dried, organic peppermint leaves for every cup of boiling water. Let it steep for half an hour and cool. When it's room temperature, you can decant it into a spray bottle. Use this outside on your plants and flowers. This prevents bugs from munching on your blooms and salad greens, although once it's washed away through rain or watering, you'll need to re-mist with the refreshing scent of peppermint.

Lavender oil also acts as a natural insect repellent. Just wipe it on any counters where ants or other insects are crawling, and they'll leave.

★

Kirsti Boothroyd, whose story of detoxing from sugar was recounted in Chapter 7, learned of the harmful effects of household chemicals. Reading the ingredient lists, she discovered toxins in her toothpaste, shampoo, conditioner, face cream, and cleaning products. She was horrified by this knowledge, as she had three small children she wanted to keep safe.

She did some research on the subject and decided to remove all chemicals from her home. She wrote on her whiteboard "Chemical-Free Home" as a commitment to the angels. She asked them for help in replacing the old chemicals. The very next day, she found enough money to replace all chemicals with Earth-conscious products.

★

A wonderful website sponsored by the Environmental Working Group will give you instant analyses of the ingredients in thousands of cosmetics, toiletries, and personal-care items. You just type in the name of the product and you'll read about any toxins it may contain. We highly recommend this website: www .ewg.org/skindeep.

In addition, Americans can download a3 app for their smartphones that allows for pointing at the UPC bar code on a food product to learn if it contains genetically modified (GMO) ingredients. Look for it in your app store under the name "Fooducate." As you set up and personalize the app, simply move the button that asks whether or not you want it to scan for GMOs (you definitely do).

Supplements and herbal products aren't exempt from chemicals and toxins. At the time of this writing, there's information coming out saying that so-called organic products from China may be contaminated with heavy metals such as lead, mercury, and cadmium. In China, there are different regulations governing organic farming. As long as the farmer isn't adding additional pesticides or fertilizers to the crops, they can be called organic. The soil or water may contain many harmful toxins, though. Most supplements and herbal products will be concentrated, and if they aren't grown in a truly organic way, there can be concentrations of toxins, too.

Check product labels and seek out organic supplements when possible. Read the labels and find out where the ingredients are sourced or where the product is manufactured. Making an informed choice leads to better health.

Items for a Healing Home

In addition to removing items from your home, here are some products you can implement for health benefits:

Water Filters and Purifiers

Check with your local water district to see if fluoride is added to the water supply. If it is, protest this archaic and dangerous practice. A lot of times cities continue to add fluoride without questioning the habit. Do research on the latest scientific information regarding fluoride health hazards, which outweigh the minimal advantages for oral health.

In the meantime, it's wise to get a water filter or purifier for your home. There are many varieties, starting with the small and inexpensive hand-held Brita or Pur brand water filters connected to a water pitcher that you keep in your refrigerator.

You can buy more elaborate water filters that fit beneath your kitchen sink to purify the water you use for tea, cooking, and drinking. Or, you can buy a whole-house reverse-osmosis system. These systems are sold in "stages," with each stage treating and filtering the water. The more stages, the cleaner the water. You may need to add minerals back into reverse-osmosis water to ensure that it's alkaline and tastes good.

Organic Fabrics

Ordinary sheets, blankets, comforters, and towels are made from synthetic oil-based materials or from pesticide-covered cotton. These materials are often made in sweatshops where workers are treated cruelly and barely paid any money. Because the manufacturers don't pay a decent wage to workers, the items are sold inexpensively at major department stores. You think you're getting a bargain, but think again. . . .

How does the energy of sleeping on sheets that are made at someone else's painful expense affect you? And if you're sleeping on synthetic sheets, have you noticed that your skin can't "breathe" and you often feel sweaty, or too hot or cold?

That's why we highly recommend investing in organic and sustainable household fabric goods that are made under Fair Trade operations (meaning that the workers are treated and paid fairly).

The positive-energy difference in sleeping with organic sheets, pillows, and blankets is huge! Sheets made from organic bamboo and cotton are soft and cuddly, like your most comfortable shirts. You may enjoy the experience so much that you gradually start wearing organic-fabric clothing, which also has a high-vibrational frequency that you can feel each time you wear it.

Organic Personal-Care Products

Only purchase organic cotton swabs, as ordinary cotton is filled with pesticides and genetic modifications. Get as much information as you can so you can rest assured that you're using safe and natural products. Search for the ethics of a brand or company to ensure they treat their workers fairly. Don't buy products from companies that use animal testing or that are fighting the labeling of GMOs. All of these factors will filter down through the energy of the items produced. You're already doing so much work on your energy and spirituality, so it makes sense to take excellent care of your physical body, too.

Infrared Saunas

Traditional saunas use a hot environment to promote sweating. They typically have a heating element of rocks that reaches a high temperature. Moisture is added to the air by pouring cupfuls of water over the stones. Infrared saunas are quite different. They do little to heat up the external environment, but work with infrared radiation to heat your body internally. These infrared saunas filter out the UV radiation, leaving behind the same infrared radiation that comes from the sun. These waves of radiation only penetrate a little way into the skin. They can help raise your metabolism and promote sweating in a safe way.

Your skin is the biggest organ of elimination. Through sweating, you can release old, built-up toxins. Infrared saunas stimulate your circulation and bring more oxygen into your cells. As this occurs, you push out chemicals and health hazards into sweat. Saunas can be great for people who don't sweat regularly through exercise. Use infrared saunas to cleanse your body if you haven't exercised for some time. This releases any buildup of toxins and encourages you to enjoy exercise again.

Start using infrared saunas slowly. Begin with 20 or 30 minutes and then get out. Over time, you can slowly increase the amount of time spent in a sauna. However, in the early stages of your detox, less is best.

An Organic Garden

This may be the most important item you could add to your healing home, for the sake of your health. Gardening is relaxing and meditative, and connects you with nature. And food grown in your own garden has the highest vibration of anything you could possibly eat! The angels say that eating freshly picked, locally grown produce is like reading Mother Earth's newspaper because you're connecting with, and getting messages about, local energies.

You don't have to own a piece of land to grow a garden—you can grow one anywhere! There are hydroponic gardening kits for sale online that allow you to create a garden inside your home. You can also plant tomatoes and other hardy vegetables in pots on your balcony.

There are many online resources and books to help you finesse your garden. There are also gardening clubs that will give you personal support and the opportunity to meet new friends. Similarly, some communities have co-op gardens, with a large plot of land subdivided between many people.

Be sure to plant only heirloom, organic, and non–genetically modified seeds. You can buy them online through reputable suppliers who've taken the "Safe Seed Pledge." This means that they're certifying that no artificial bioengineering has touched their seeds. Heirloom and organic seeds can be harvested for other seasons. GMO seeds have been created to only last one season, forcing gardeners and farmers to give money to GMO corporations for new crops.

★ ★ ★

AFTERWORD

Treat your body as the precious temple it is. It houses your sacred soul, which is eternally bright. You only get one body per lifetime, so take care of it! Your body is your primary tool for your Divine life mission, so it's essential you treat it right. Detox your life with the guidance of the angels, and your light will shine.

Others will notice your high energy and want to know how you attained it. They might ask, "What's your secret?" There's no secret—you're not keeping anything from these people. You've simply chosen to treat your body with the respect it deserves. Taking excellent care of yourself physically, emotionally, and spiritually benefits everyone!

— Doreen and Robert

★ ★ ★

BIBLIOGRAPHY

V De Re, L Caggiari, M Tabuso, R Cannizzaro. "The versatile role of gliadin pep-
tides in celiac disease." *Clin Biochem.* 2012. Clinical and Experimental Pharmacol-
ogy. Centro di Riferimento Oncologico. IRCCS, National Cancer Institute, Italy.

N Eriksson, S Wu, C B Do, A K Kiefer, J Y Tung, J L Mountain, D A Hinds,
U Francke. "A genetic variant near olfactory receptor genes influences cilantro
preference." *Flavour.* November 29, 2012.

★ ★ ★

ABOUT THE AUTHORS

Doreen Virtue holds B.A., M.A., and Ph.D. degrees in counseling psychology. As a former psychotherapist, Doreen has helped clients detox from alcohol, drugs, and food addictions in inpatient hospital and outpatient settings. With the assistance of the angels, Doreen was guided many years ago to give up all alcohol, coffee, refined sugar, and animal products; and to live an organic, sober, vegan lifestyle, which she credits for her high energy and youthful spirit. Doreen has also written about detoxing in her books *The Art of Raw Living Food, Healing with the Angels,* and *The Angel Therapy Handbook.*

Doreen has appeared on *Oprah,* CNN, *The View,* and other television and radio programs and writes regular columns for *Woman's World* magazine. Her products are available in most languages worldwide, on Kindle and other eBook platforms, and as iTunes apps. For more information on Doreen and the workshops she presents, please visit: www.AngelTherapy.com.

You can listen to Doreen's live weekly radio show, and call her for a reading, by visiting HayHouseRadio.com®.

ANGEL THERAPY®

Robert Reeves, N.D., is an accredited naturopath who blends his herbal medicine and nutrition training with his psychic and mediumship abilities. He has a strong connection to the angels and to the natural world, believing that nature holds Divine healing properties. Robert feels we can all benefit from living a more natural life.

Robert gives self-help and spiritual-development workshops, writes magazine articles, and has been featured on international radio programs. He owns and runs a successful natural-therapies clinic in Australia, which he began when he was 17 years old. He has also developed a range of vibrational essences focusing on crystal and angel energy, which are currently available as aura sprays. Robert is co-author, with Doreen, of *Living Pain-Free, Flower Therapy,* and *Flower Therapy Oracle Cards.*

For more information about Robert, please visit: www.Robert Reeves.com.au.

★ ★ ★

NOTES

NOTES

NOTES

NOTES

NOTES

Hay House Titles of Related Interest

YOU CAN HEAL YOUR LIFE, the movie, starring Louise Hay & Friends
(available as a 1-DVD program and an expanded 2-DVD set)
Watch the trailer at: www.LouiseHayMovie.com

THE SHIFT, the movie,
starring Dr. Wayne W. Dyer
(available as a 1-DVD program and an expanded 2-DVD set)
Watch the trailer at: www.DyerMovie.com

★

CRAZY SEXY KITCHEN: 150 Plant-Empowered Recipes to Ignite a Mouthwatering Revolution, by Kris Carr, with Chef Chris Sarno

HEALING WITH RAW FOODS: Your Guide to Unlocking Vibrant Health Through Living Cuisine, by Jenny Ross
INTEGRATIVE WELLNESS RULES: A Simple Guide to Healthy Living, by Dr. Jim Nicolai

MEALS THAT HEAL INFLAMMATION: Embrace Healthy Living and Eliminate Pain, One Meal at a Time, by Julie Daniluk, R.H.N.

MINDFUL EATING, by Miraval

All of the above are available at your local bookstore,
or may be ordered by contacting Hay House (see next page).

★

We hope you enjoyed this Hay House book. If you'd like
to receive our online catalog featuring additional information on
Hay House books and products, or if you'd like to find out more
about the Hay Foundation, please contact:

Hay House, Inc., P.O. Box 5100, Carlsbad, CA 92018-5100
(760) 431-7695 or (800) 654-5126
(760) 431-6948 (fax) or (800) 650-5115 (fax)
www.hayhouse.com® • www.hayfoundation.org

★

Published and distributed in Australia by: Hay House Australia Pty. Ltd.,
18/36 Ralph St., Alexandria NSW 2015 • *Phone:* 612-9669-4299
Fax: 612-9669-4144 • www.hayhouse.com.au

Published and distributed in the United Kingdom by: Hay House UK, Ltd.,
Astley House, 33 Notting Hill Gate, London W11 3JQ • *Phone:* 44-20-3675-2450
Fax: 44-20-3675-2451 • www.hayhouse.co.uk

Published and distributed in the Republic of South Africa by: Hay House SA
(Pty), Ltd., P.O. Box 990, Witkoppen 2068 • *Phone/Fax:* 27-11-467-8904
www.hayhouse.co.za

Published in India by: Hay House Publishers India, Muskaan Complex,
Plot No. 3, B-2, Vasant Kunj, New Delhi 110 070 • *Phone:* 91-11-4176-1620
Fax: 91-11-4176-1630 • www.hayhouse.co.in

Distributed in Canada by: Raincoast Books,
2440 Viking Way, Richmond, B.C. V6V 1N2
Phone: 1-800-663-5714 • *Fax:* 1-800-565-3770 • www.raincoast.com

★

Take Your Soul on a Vacation

Visit www.HealYourLife.com® to regroup, recharge,
and reconnect with your own magnificence.
Featuring blogs, mind-body-spirit news, and life-changing
wisdom from Louise Hay and friends.

Visit www.HealYourLife.com today!

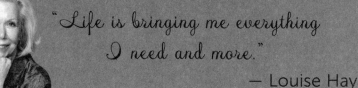